Sing *of* Life

Revisioning
Tagore's *Gitanjali*

PRIYA
SARUKKAI CHABRIA

cntxt

First published in hardback by Context, an imprint of Westland Publications Private Limited, in 2021

Published in paperback by Context, an imprint of Westland Books, a division of Nasadiya Technologies Private Limited, in 2024

No. 269/2B, First Floor, 'Irai Arul', Vimalraj Street, Nethaji Nagar, Alapakkam Main Road, Maduravoyal, Chennai 600095

Westland, the Westland logo, Context and the Context logo are the trademarks of Nasadiya Technologies Private Limited, or its affiliates.

ISBN: 9789360451448

10 9 8 7 6 5 4 3 2 1

Typeset by Jojy Philip, New Delhi
Printed at [ ]

Sing *of* Life

Priya Sarukkai Chabria is an award-winning poet, translator and writer of ten books of poetry, speculative fiction, literary non-fiction and translation and, as editor, three poetry anthologies. Her books include *Andal: The Autobiography of a Goddess* (translation), *Calling Over Water* (poems), *Clone* (speculative fiction) and *Bombay/ Mumbai: Immersions* (non-fiction).

Priya channels Sanskrit aesthetic theory and ancient Tamil poetics into her writing. As Founding Editor, Poetry at Sangam (http:// poetryatsangam.com) she is currently editing the anthology *Fafnir's Heart World Poetry in Translation*. She is the recipient of the Muse Translation Award, Kitab Experimental Fiction Award and Best Reads by Feminist Press, and has been recognised for her Outstanding Contribution to Literature by the Government of India. Her work has been widely anthologised and translated into Indian and European languages. Forthcoming are her memoir, *Archive of Absences*, and translations of the Tamil mystic Manikkavacagar.

Priya is on the advisory council of WrICE Writers Immersion and Cultural Exchange, Australia. www.priyasarukkaichabria.com.

Introduction

Spring morning, Bir, Himachal Pradesh.
Ahead, snowcapped mountains.
Above, wheeling paragliders.
Around, crisp sunlight.

Under such a sky I begin reading *Gitanjali (Song Offering)* by Rabindranath Tagore, subtitled *A Collection of Prose Translations Made by the Author from the Original Bengali with an Introduction by W.B. Yeats* and first published in 1913.

My reading starts as a casual glance at the book my husband picked off a café bookshelf while we waited for our coffee. By the time we finish, the small book is spreadeagled between us. When we leave, the borrowed book comes with us, to the photocopier's.

I am tingling with elation. As I read, or rather plunge into it, certain words from each of the *Songs* lift like swans into my mind. Back in our hotel room, I write these risen phrases in the children's notebook I'd purchased at the photocopier's.

I have never begun a writing project with less preparation. I don't have a name for it. Doesn't matter. That will come later. After the birthing. As with life.

––

With its publication in English, Tagore became the first non-European to win a Nobel Prize for Literature. The Committee's citation summed up their reasons: '… because of his profoundly sensitive, fresh and beautiful verse, by which, with consummate skill, he has made his poetic thought, expressed in his own English words, a part of the literature of the West.' I hadn't read the Bengali visionary and educationist at any length before, though he produced prodigious amounts of poetry, prose, drama and fiction in his lifetime (7 May 1861–7 August 1941). His fame and the awe in which he is held formed an almost impenetrable aura around him. 'Gurudev, Teacher embodying God-like knowledge' was the sobriquet conferred on him by M. K. Gandhi, while he, in turn, bestowed the appellation 'Mahatma' on Gandhi. The Bengali claim on Tagore made me feel in part an interloper, part *parvenu*, part *weisenheimer*, when I attempted any more than a nodding acquaintance with his books. Yet, I cherished the cinematic adaptations of his works,[*] and had pored over his haunting paintings and doodles;[**] my approach to his work was at an angle. And now, suddenly, to my surprise, I was immersed in rewriting his best-known work.

The impetus perhaps rests in this verse from the *Upanishads*, translated by Tagore:

From joy does spring all this creation, by joy is it maintained, towards joy does it progress, and into joy does it enter.

— —

My encounter with the *Gitanjali* splits, like forked lightning, into two spaces.

There is Tagore's own historical moment as the anti-colonial struggle was gathering force, and his part in the nationalist upsurge. He wrote from a position of great privilege within the reformist Brahmo Samaj movement in Calcutta, British India's capital. His inner

---

[*] Satyajit Ray's *Charulata* (1964), *Teen Kanya* (1961), *Ghare Baire* (1984) and the documentary *Rabindranath Tagore* made to mark Gurudev's 150th birth centenary in 1961, Kumar Shahani's *Char Adhyay* (1997), Hemant Gupta's *Kabuliwala* (1961), Suman Mukhopadhyay's *Chaturanga*, Nitin Bose's *Milan* (1946), Tapan Sinha's *Kshudhita Pashan* (1960), Gulzar's *Lekin* (1991), Hiren Nag's *Geet Gaata Chal* (1975), Sudhendu Roy's *Uphaar* (1971) and Deb Medhekar's *Bioscopewala* (2018).

[**] https://theculturetrip.com/asia/india/articles/the-underappreciated-paintings-of-rabindranath-tagore/, http://ngmaindia.gov.in/sh-rabindranath.asp

need for his work to be acknowledged by friends and admirers among the intellectual elite in India and the West propelled him. Underlying this was the voice of Bengal's riverine culture, which quivered within him as he sailed through pastoral landscapes; he was also seeking to transmute grief over the death of close family members into the grace of acceptance. These currents poured into his profound meditations on life and death and overflowed as the *Gitanjali*.

Now, to my particular moment. As I held the book to me, it opened like a treasure chest's maw of light. After I completed the re-writing, I began the research that revealed serendipitous correlations between Tagore's thinking and my intuited choices. Some of the poems spilled like blessings. Others were like lip-splitting experiences, tasting of blood and birth. Coincidences, or something else altogether, led me into a new cave of understanding, another vault to explore.

— —

At fifteen I remember being taught the *Gitanjali's* justly celebrated Song 35:

Where the mind is without fear and the head is held high;
Where knowledge is free;
Where the world has not been broken up into fragments by narrow
domestic walls;
Where words come out from the depth of truth;
Where tireless striving stretches its arms towards perfection;
Where the clear stream of reason has not lost its way into the dreary
desert sand of dead habit;
Where the mind is led forward by thee into ever-widening thought
and action—
Into that heaven of freedom, my Father, let my country awake.

I remember being stirred; I remember thinking: This is beautiful, but rather wordy. I want to hear the *Gitanjali* in the patois of the present. I had just discovered e e cummings, who, though merely a generation younger than Tagore, experimented radically with language and form.

—

Post-colonial historical narratives make us familiar with the idea of prominent intellectuals like Tagore and Ram Mohan Roy, who (though they resisted this as well) partially became pens in spreading the knowledge discourses of the British. Tagore was a cornerstone of the Bengal Renaissance while Yeats figured prominently in the Irish Literary Revival of the late 1800s; both men were aware of the 'potency of their artistic representations of their nations during a charged political time'[*] and, indeed, their pivotal roles in the era's East–West cultural encounters, however uneven this may have been.

Tagore, in many ways, accepts the role accorded to him by the West: the spiritually minded, other-worldly, inward-looking Oriental. Western intellectuals delight in their blinkered vision of his complex and energising personality, and he, in turn, is taken up with the reception he receives. 'Those who know the English only in India, do not know Englishmen,' he declares. 'All you people live, think and talk while a strong, critical light is constantly focussed on you. This creates a high social civilisation. We in India, on the contrary, live secluded among a crowd of relations. Things are done and said within the family circle which would not be tolerated outside; and this keeps our social standards low.'[**] He enhances his persona as a seeker of the sacred by wearing the markers of the Eastern sage: the long beard, the long robe or jobba that he designed for himself. It drapes well, and falls from his shoulders like the mantel of a wizard.

---

[*] Krishna Dutta and Andrew Robinson (eds.), *Selected Letters of Rabindranath Tagore*, Cambridge University Press, 1997. Letter published in *Modern Review*, Calcutta, July 1919.

[**] William Rothenstein, 'Rabindranath Tagore in London', https://fortnightlyreview.co.uk/2013/05/tagore-in-london/

Perhaps he fashions himself, to a degree, after the nineteenth-century monk, Swami Vivekananda, who was instrumental in spreading Hindu spirituality and yoga to the West even as he promoted Indian nationalism. He had his robes designed for him, including the swanky turban, to cut a striking figure as a sage. Tagore tells the French Nobel laureate for Literature, Romain Rolland, 'If you want to know India, study Vivekananda. In him everything is positive and nothing negative.'

Not so with Tagore. He has his demons. At times, he seems to lacerate himself with self-doubt. He sees himself as a nationalist, and then again, not. He disagrees with the potential violence in any nationalist movement; he is prescient and sees the gag effect it could have on a nation's means of expression. He steps back. As Ranjit Hoskote suggests, he was 'moving at a tangent to the centre of their (his) civilisations, even at the risk of being misunderstood.'*

Tagore sees contesting reflections. As if he is on a boat, peering into the river's flow. But each time he peers, the reflections reshape clearer. He takes it upon himself to 're-educate' his colonial friends with a corrective course on Indian culture, as is evident in this passage from *Sadhana: The Realisation of Life*:** 'The west seems to take a pride in thinking that it is subduing nature; as if we are living in a hostile world where we have to wrest everything we want from an unwilling and alien arrangement of things … India put all her emphasis on the harmony that exists between the individual and the universal. She felt we could have no communication whatever with our surroundings if they were absolutely foreign to us.'

—–

* Ranjit Hoskote, 'Walking Through Mirrors? Reflections on the Spiritual Traffic Between India and Europe', in Angelika Fitz, Merle Kröger, Alexandra Schneider and Dorothee Wenner (eds.), *Import Export: Cultural Transfer, India, Germany, Austria*, Parthas Verlag, Berlin, 2005.
** Rabindranath Tagore, *Sādhanā: The Realisation of Life*, Macmillan & Co., London, 1913 & 1957.

Tagore seeks to renew traditional aesthetic modes. At the same time, he engages with Western aesthetic practices and arguments. Again, rather than imitate or reject, he absorbs those that further his syncretic understanding of the world and himself within it, the landscapes opening wider and wider within him. 'One must bear in mind that those who have the true modern spirit need not modernise, just as those who are truly brave are not braggarts ... True modernism is freedom of mind, not slavery of taste. It is independence of thought and action, not tutelage under European schoolmasters ...'*

His path is singular; he does not burn the grass behind him as much as shine the fierce light of his moral reasoning on it, so that the grass still shimmers with life in his wake.

—

To my mind, Tagore is a modernist bhakti/devotional poet. Cosmic harmonies ring through the love that souses this collection, at once familiar and mysterious as the changing lines on one's palm. A blessed geography of space is summoned from within the body's cells and outside, and in every time, whether recollected, in the present, or yet to come.

His address to the Beloved is intimate, whether anguished or brimming with gratitude; it is at all times as enveloping as a skin. Pioneering art historian Ananda K. Coomaraswamy declared in *The Dance of Shiva: Fourteen Indian Essays*, 'Rabindranath Tagore is the latest singer' of this passionate devotional mode in which '... was complete the cycle of Indian spiritual evolution from pure

---

* *'While I agree ... so far as to say that the spirit of the race should harmonise with the spirit of the times, I must warn ... that modernising is a mere affectation of modernism, just as affectation of poesy is poetising. It is nothing but mimicry, only affectation is louder than the original, and it is too literal ...'* Rabindrananth Tagore, quoted in *Planeta Literatur: Journal of Global Literary Studies*, No. 3, 2014.

philosophy to pure mysticism, from knowledge to love. The inner and outer life were finally unified…'*

Numerous markers of bhakti poetry are strewn throughout the *Gitanjali*, like green leaves peeking through a rose garland, discreet but enriching the pattern.

An osmosis of gendering, in which male and female identities pass through the membrane of the imagination, occurs and reoccurs. As for instance, in Song 52 he sings, 'You depart. I find /on the bed a petal. I find / / your sword heavy as a bolt /of thunder.'

From Sanskrit poetics Tagore draws the concept of the wandering abhisarika nayika, who plunges into the stormy night and the darkness of doubt to meet her Beloved. This lends itself to bhakti's insatiable cravings, as in this fragment from Song 94: 'I start my journey with /empty hands, expectant heart. // Though / there are dangers, I have no fear.' The journey darkens, but as in Song 91, death is the auspicious bride who waits with the garland that will free the bridegroom, the author, and by extension, us. 'The garland is ready for the bridegroom,' he writes. Death replenishes 'the pitcher of life'; it is the last fulfilment of life. Towards the end of *Gitanjali*, Tagore craves this experience: to be restored, by death, to his original home.

Sometimes Rabindranath Tagore is a beggar girl who pulls her dusty skirt over her head. Her presence has haunted him since his teenage years; this image of him wounds us.

— —

I read that Tagore wrote in 'the common language of the people'— as did the subcontinent's medieval mystics, who preferred to sing in their mother tongue over courtly and sanctified Sanskrit. Apparently,

---

* Ananda K. Coomaraswamy, *The Dance of Shiva: Fourteen Indian Essays with an Introductory Preface by Romain Rolland*, Munshiram Manoharlal Publishers Pvt. Ltd, Delhi, 2009.

this 'lowering' of literary language was not well accepted by Indian critics of his time. Also, like the medieval mystics, he pushed towards social reform and democratisation of India's feudal order. In May 1919, after the massacre in April of unarmed civilians by the British Indian Army in Jallianwala Bagh, an anguished Tagore returned his knighthood. 'The time has come when badges of honour make our shame glaring in their incongruous context of humiliation, and I for my part wish to stand, shorn of all special distinctions, by the side of my country men,' he wrote to Lord Chelmsford, Viceroy of India. He cut free of any cloud of imperialist complicity.

—-—

The *Gitanjali*'s structure is both moored and unmoored; it unmoors us from our tethering ropes. It drifts between exultation, self-abnegation, despair and wonder as Tagore craves to dissolve into the 'Ineffable Person'. This craving sparkles like sunlight on water through his use of repetition and refrains. His locations move too, rippling from riverbank to temple, market to home, while he voyages between the self, an idyllic village life, the river and its cross-currents. He throbs for deliverance through detachment, not renunciation. All the while, he also writes about the act of writing, as in Songs 66, 75, 84, 101, 102, and on making music—while, in a sense, being made into music himself. 'Art is the response of man's creative soul to the call of the Real,' he declares.

Art is his path to spiritual transcendence; an ode to all that lives, lingers and vanishes, and that which remains after all else has vanished. India's philosopher President, Dr Sarvepalli Radhakrishnan wrote, 'The poems of *Gitanjali* are the offerings of the finite to the infinite.'

Some call the book Tagore's autobiography.

—-—

Without my being aware, while writing this book, Rabindranath Tagore silently transmutes to Gurudev, like a new moon growing full, rounding into luminescence, revealingly its true nature.

—–

In his dreams, does he wander after Bauls who sing mystical new paths into existence?

—–

Everything calls to him. The sad music of the water, dusk, by-lanes and paths on water too, as in Song 74:

at

> the fording

> > in a boat

> > > an unknown man

plays on his lute

In Tagore studies, the 'unknown man' is often interpreted as the Divine. This links to his Vaishnava culture where God is the alluring flute player who leads us into the lila-play of the world and leads us out of it as well. He, then, is the musical instrument played upon by the 'Master Musician'. Gurudev's questing could also be the melody, its shape.

Or the boat could be his body, the boatman his own self, who he seeks to know better through his music and writings.

Or is he suggesting that the 'unknown man' is each one of us, solitary and star-like, floating on the boat of her life? The correct answer may be all three, and more. Gurudev loathed merely literal interpretations and abhorred corrals of any kind.

He is a flagship, minus an armada, sailing on indigo seas, moonlit.

—–

What are the *Lakshman Rekhas*, the limits, one must not cross when working in Tagore's terrain? Simultaneously, what are the boundaries one must build so that Gurudev doesn't swamp one's own creativity and individuality? Rigour and license don't oppose each other; they course together.

On that first day in Bir, as I put pencil to paper, I decide I will not alter his word order, nor interpolate, nor substitute his words; I will stay with the present tense to honour the work's energy.

I stay with the thrall.

—–

I shift his employment of the archaic 'Thou-Thee-Thine' into the familiarity of 'you-yours' which comes to me from my translating bhakti poetry; also, as the *Gitanjali* follows in this tradition. The use of lofty language led to a certain rigidity, not rigour; fossilising the words, not freeing their flow. This did not agree with my translator's urge, which is to not merely decode the original, but *re-code* with intensity, immediacy and creativity, so words pulse through the reader's being.

—–

At the inception, I had no idea that Gurudev's theories on translation and re-writing would splendidly confirm my own intuited choices. But I found, time and again, that his arguments and meditations segued into my self-imposed rules. Each new finding was like an anchor, each one a spike of elation. The experience was like nectar being tipped back into the flower's calyx. I was brimming.

—–

The original Bengali *Gitanjali* was published on 14 August 1910 by Indian Publishing House, 22 Cornwallis Street, Calcutta. For this, he wrote fifty new poems, culled the rest from his works, *Naivédya,*

Khéya and *Gitimala*, and added some poems which had earlier appeared in periodicals. The English *Gitanjali* was first published in November 1912 by the Indian Society of London. The Bengali poems, numbering 156 or 157—depending on how one looks at it—were whittled down to 103 prose translations. He edited out fifty poems. But why the confusion about the number 156 or 157? He fused two separate poems, 89 and 90, of the *Naivédya* into one, which we now know as 95. The work was his to transform. Re-make. Re-present.

—–—

'When you change the way you look at things, the things you look at change' states the quantum physicist Max Planck. William Blake shifts the focus somewhat when he says, 'As a man is, so he sees.' Both these reflections stay with me as I work on the *Gitanjali*.

Initially, I was briefly persuaded to term a published excerpt as my 'erasure' poems of the *Gitanjali*. Though erasure is a form of contained writing, its reductionist connotations didn't agree with me, for mine is a tribute. Besides, I believe a great poem is one that often serves as a draft or raft for someone else's poem. Or that is how it should be: A spark or a shift in another's subconscious.

A friend suggested I was 'vivifying' Gurudev's twentieth-century prose translations into twenty-first-century poetry. But wasn't I, smitten by the work, simultaneously getting vivified? After completing all 103 poems, I re-read the *Gitanjali*. It still swam in me like an electric eel; it had more to offer. I found 'remainder' poems floating within each of the *Song Offerings*. The intense longing that swarmed through Gurudev when he was writing surged in me too, almost beyond articulation. These fragments are, to me, not an exercise in asceticism, rather an intensification of emotion. They are not sundered, they are rather sculptural offerings. Stammers towards the sacred. Song 34:

i

name

you

my all

come

to you

in

everything

—–

'Macmillan's are urging me to send them some translations of my short stories,' Tagore writes to his friend, the influential critic and lithographer William Rothenstein. 'They require rewriting in English, not translating.'[*] Almost 70 years before the term 'translation studies' was coined, Tagore was a largely unacknowledged pioneer in theorising the field. He saw it as a 'thing' worth studying, an independent discipline rather than an exercise in learning a foreign language; as a creative process rather than a mechanical practice.

—–

In the Preface to *The Gardener* (1913)[**] which Tagore dedicated to Yeats, he declares, 'Most of the lyrics of love and life, the translations of which from Bengali are published in this book, were written much earlier than the series of religious poems contained in the book named *Gitanjali*. The translations are not always literal, the originals being sometimes abridged and sometimes paraphrased.' Again, *The Gardener* is a work of self-translation, doubly so, for it is translated

---

[*] Mary Lago (ed.), *Imperfect Encounter: Letters of William Rothenstein and Rabindranath Tagore: 1911–1941*, Cambridge University Press, 1972.

[**] Rabindranath Tagore, *The Gardener* (tr. by the author from the Bengali), Macmillan & Co., London, 1913.

from one language into another and because, for him, translation necessitated rewriting sections as well as condensing the original. In this, Gurudev was true to the Indic tradition of translation and transmission which acknowledges that diverse versions of a source text do not lack fidelity but each is held as equally valid. As I read his words, I felt a deep comfort.

Similarly, after completing my work on the *Gitanjali,* I found another serendipitous connection in this passage from *Glimpses of Bengal.*[*] These are letters he wrote between 1885 and 1895, in particular to his niece, Indiradevi Chaudharini, as he travelled, often in his family's luxurious houseboat, on the slow, sparkling river Padma, to inspect the outlying areas of his ancestral properties.

BOLPUR *19th October 1894.*

We know people only in dotted outline, that is to say, with gaps in our knowledge which we have to fill in ourselves, as best we can. Thus, even those we know well are largely made up of our imagination. Sometimes the lines are so broken, with even the guiding dots missing, that a portion of the picture remains darkly confused and uncertain. If, then, our best friends are only pieces of broken outline strung on a thread of imagination, do we really know anybody at all, or does anybody know us except in the same disjointed fashion? But perhaps it is these very loopholes, allowing entrance to each other's imagination, which make for intimacy; otherwise each one, secure in his inviolate individuality, would have been unapproachable to all but the Dweller within. Our own self, too, we know only in bits, and with these scraps of material we have to shape the hero of our lifestory—likewise with

---

[*] *Glimpses of Bengal: Selected from the Letters of Sir Rabindranath Tagore, 1885 to 1895,* Macmillan & Co, London; digitised by the Internet Archive in 2007 with funding from Microsoft Corporation, http://www.archive.org/details/glimpsesofbenga100tagoiala.

the help of our imagination. Providence has, doubtless, deliberately omitted portions so that we may assist in our own creation.

What we know is partial, of ourselves and others. For what we perceive are dotted outlines. Specks of light are outlined by imagination and grace. Wholeness is only a suggestion.

We assist in our own creation, and creations. Each one, individually, creates.

Dotted outlines of personalities across oceans and positions taken on various cultural questions connect Gurudev to several of his contemporaries, among them, Romain Roland, Yeats, Coomaraswamy, Einstein and the Mahatma.

––

Below is Gurudev's Song 96. Phrases in **bold** comprise my first poem, the underlined sections become my second poem.

When I go from hence let this be my parting word, that what I have seen is unsurpassable.
*<u>I have tasted</u> of the <u>hidden honey</u> of this lotus that expands on the ocean of light, and thus **am I blessed** – let this be my parting word.*
In** this playhouse of **infinite forms I have** had my play and here have **I caught sight of** him **that is formless.
<u>My</u> whole <u>body</u> and my limbs have <u>thrilled with his touch who is beyond touch</u>; and if the end comes here, let it come – let this be my parting word.

When I go
let this be my parting word

what I have seen
is unsurpassable

Am I blessed

*In infinite forms I have caught
sight of that formless*

—–—

i

have tasted

hidden honey

my body

thrills

with his touch

who is

beyond

touch

—–—

In its last poem, Song 85 of *The Gardener,* Gurudev prefigures my urge to remake his words a hundred years later.

Who are you, reader, reading my poems an hundred years hence?

I cannot send you one single flower from this wealth of the spring, one single streak of gold from yonder clouds.

Open your doors and look abroad.

From your blossoming garden gather fragrant memories of the vanished flowers of an hundred years before.

In the joy of your heart may you feel the living joy that sang one spring morning, sending its glad voice across an hundred years…

We hear:

call me

       from sleep

              lead me

running

          from glade

                  to glade

Sing of Life

Gitanjali

Introduction by William Butler Yeats, September 1912

Other Indians came to see me.
Their reverence / for this man sounded
strange / in our world. When / we were
making the cathedrals / had we a like

reverence /for our great men? /The other day
the curator of a museum/ pointed
out to me a little dark-skinned man/ who
was arranging their Chinese prints:'*That/*

is the hereditary connoisseur
of the Mikado/ he
is the fourteenth of
his family/ to hold the post.' /

I thought
of the abundance / of
the simplicity
of these poems. /

These prose translations/ have stirred
my heart. / (I have carried
the manuscript about me for days!) /
These lyrics / display

in their thoughts / a world/
I had dreamed of all my life long./
The work of a supreme
culture / yet they appear / as

much the growth of the common
soil / as the grass and the rushes. /
A tradition where poetry and religion / are
the same thing, /

passed through centuries. /
These verses will not lie /
in little well-printed books /
upon ladies' tables who turn /
the pages with indolent / hands
that they may sigh over a life / without
meaning / which is yet all
they can know / about life. /

A whole civilisation/ immeasurably
strange to us/ seems to have
been taken/ up into this imagination. /
Yet we are not moved/

because of its strangeness/ but
because/ we have met our own
image/ as though/ perhaps for the first
time/ in literature / our voice as in

a dream. / We know we must /
forsake at last this world/ but
how can we who have read
so much poetry/ seen

so many paintings/ listened
to so much music where/ the cry
of the flesh and/ the cry of the soul
seem one/ forsake it?

What have we in common? /
Yet/ looking backward/ upon our

life/ we discover / that emotion that/
created this insidious sweetness. /

This is no/ longer
the sanctity of the cell and/
of the scourage/ being
lifted/ into a greater intensity/ and

we go/ for a like voice to
St. Francis and/ to William Blake/ who
have seemed so alien
to our violent history. /

Mr Tagore, like Indian civilisation
itself, / has been content/ to
discover the soul / and surrender
himself / to its spontaneity: /

An innocence / a simplicity that
one does not find/ elsewhere
in literature /
makes the birds and the leaves

seems as near to him /
as they are near to children /…

(On 27 June 1912, at the home of William Rothenstein, Rabindranath Tagore and William Butler Yeats meet face-to-face for the first time, after Yeats read Tagore's partial translation of the *Gitanjali*. This marked the beginning of a literary friendship which, in hindsight, seems more on Yeats's part than Tagore's. Yeats went through the *Gitanjali* and suggested edits. This encounter also produced Yeats's fulsome 'Introduction' for a grateful Tagore. Both won the Nobel Prize: Tagore in 1913, and Yeats a decade later in 1923.

Twenty-three years after the *Gitanjali* was published, in May 1935, Yeats wrote to Rothenstein: 'Damn Tagore. We got out three good books, [poet Thomas] Sturge Moore and I, because he thought it more important to see and know English than to be a great poet, he brought out sentimental rubbish and wrecked his reputation. Tagore does not know English, no Indian can know English.')[*]

[*] https://scholarblogs.emory.edu/postcolonialstudies/2020/02/16/yeats-w-b-india-and-rabindranath-tagore/

1

Endless pleasure
gives birth to utterance

Gifts come
to these small hands of mine

Ages pass
and still you pour   still

there is room to fill

— —

                              vessel

                    empties

               and empties

       again

and fills

this flute

of a reed

          breathes

            melodies

               and pours

2

To sing
it seems my heart would break

All that is harsh and dissolute melts   spreads
wings across the sky

My song reaches
the joy of singing

— —

tears
sweet harmony

glad bird

        on its flight

                across the sea

                        drunk

i forget myself

3

I listen in silent amazement
Light illumines the world   runs

from sky to sky
breaks through

My heart struggles for a voice
in endless meshes of music

——

breath

streams

breaks

obstacles

         rushes on

     my heart

captive

     in the endless

4

Life of my life
I shall try to keep my body

pure   Keep untruths out   kindle
light in my mind   drive evil away   keep

my love
in flower in the shrine of my heart

--

your

      living touch

on all

my limbs

5

I ask for a moment
The works I have in hand I will finish

My heart knows no rest   My work
becomes endless in a shoreless sea

Summer has come to my window
the bees the flowering grove   Time

to sit still   face-to-face   to sing
of life in silent leisure

sing   of life   overflowing

6

Pluck this little flower
honour it with a touch of pain

The time of offering goes by
pluck it while there is time

— —

this flower

    may not find

        a place

          in a garland

       its colour

     is not

    deep

   its smell

is faint

use it

7

Make my life
like a flute of reed
to fill with music

——

put off

     adornments

        dress

           decoration

     ornaments

   come

between

you&me

8

The child decked with
prince's robes   jewelled chains

loses all pleasure in his play
keeps himself shut off

fear

that

it may fray

      be stained

            afraid

even

to move

        robbed

           of entrance

9

Come to beg

Never look back

                                         —-

                                              desire

puts out

the light

it touches

10

Where live the poorest and lowliest and lost? I
try to bow   reach down to the depth among the poorest

and lowliest and lost   My heart can never find its way
among the poorest the lowliest and the lost

— —

your   feet

rest

among the lost

     you walk

        in the clothes

          of the humble

             to find my way

       to you

     keeping company

with the lost

11

Leave chanting singing and telling of beads
 in a temple with doors shut   The tiller is

tilling the hard ground   the pathmaker is breaking
stones in sun and in shower   garment covered with dust

He is bound with us   Leave
flowers and incense   Stand by him in toil

--

who

do you worship?

where

is

deliverance?

12

The way is long

On the first light through the wilderness
leaving my track on star and planet

The most distant course comes the nearest
The most intricate leads to simplicity

Knock at every door to come to his   Wander
through outer worlds to reach the innermost

Eyes stray   I shut them   say '*Here*'
Melt into tears   Deluge the world

I am

——

my journey

to reach   the shrine

13

I spent my days stringing and
unstringing my instrument   The agony

of wishing   Blossom has not opened   wind
 is sighing   Not seen his face   listened to

his voice   Lamp has not been lit

I live in the hope of meeting

— —

the song

            i   came to sing

remains

14

My desires are many   Save
me by hard refusals

Day by day these gifts   this
sky and light and this body and the life and the mind

Day by day refusing me   saving me

— —

i linger

    i hurry

        in search

you

hide

yourself

15

I am here to sing   I have
a corner seat   I have no work to do

At the dark temple at midnight
command me to sing

In the morning air
honour my presence

— —

when

the golden harp

        is tuned

command

me

16

I have an invitation to this world's festival
Eyes have seen   ears have heard

To play upon my instrument I have
done all I could   Has the time come?

——

                                                                may

                                              i

                                                                    see

your face?

17

Waiting for love
to give myself up

Why is it so late?
Bind me fast

Waiting for love
   to his hands

Market day is over
Work is done

Those who came to call
have gone back

Waiting for love
   into his hands

——

              waiting

for his hands

18

Cloud heaps on cloud   It darkens
At the door   all alone

These lonely long
rainy hours   Gloom

Heart wanders wailing with
the restless wind

——

                              love

how

am i

to pass?

19

I will fill my heart with silence   Endure
it   I will wait like the night its head bent

low   Morning will come   golden streams breaking
their way through sky   Words will wing

from my every bird's nest   Melodies will break
in flowers in my forest groves

— —

       keep still

       starry vigil

darkness

will vanish

  your words

   will pour

20

On the day the lotus
bloomed   my mind was straying   Sadness fell

Started from my dream   Sweet trance   A
strange fragrance with the south wind

Ache

--

vague sweetness

       eager breath

           seeking

completion

  blossoms

21

I must launch my boat   Spring
has done its flowering   I wait

Yellow leaves flutter
and fall   What emptiness

A thrill through the air   notes
floating from the other shore

— —

what

do you

gaze on?

22

Deep shadows of rainy July
Morning has closed its eyes   a thick veil

over the blue   Woodlands have
hushed   Doors are shut   Solitary wayfarer

the gates are open
in my house   Do not pass by

like a dream

——

with secret steps

                    you walk

                         silent as night

eluding

        all watchers

                    loud east wind

                    deserted street

23

Stormy night   The sky groans   No
sleep   I open my door to

darkness   See nothing
By dim shore of the ink-black

river   far edge of the forest   through
gloom you come to me

——

love

where

lies

your path?

what

mazy depth

do you thread?

24

If the day is done   birds
sing no more   the wind

has flagged   draw darkness
over me   wrap earth with sleep

From the traveller   sack empty
before the voyage has ended

strength exhausted   remove
poverty

— —

you close

the petals

of the lotus

at dusk

       renew life

   like a flower

under cover

   of night

Night of weariness
Let me give

myself up to sleep
without struggle   Rest

Veil night on the tired
eyes of day

Renew sight
in fresh awakening

—-

    let

     me not

       force

my spirit

into worship

26

He sat by my side
But I... Cursed sleep

Harp in his hands   My dreams
became resonate with melodies

Are my nights all lost?
I miss his sight

—–

night is still

his

breath

                touches

my sleep

27

Where is the light?
Kindle it

Sky overcast   Ceaseless
rain   What stirs me?

Lightning drags
a deeper gloom

My heart gropes for music

Where is the light?
Kindle desire

Thunder   Wind screaming
through the void

Night black
as a black stone

Hours pass
Kindle love

——

                    never

                        a flicker

                              in the flame

                    what

does it mean

28

Freedom
is all I want

To sweep away the tinsel
that fills my room   A shroud

of dust and death
I hate it   hug it

My shame secret and
heavy   I quake

in fear lest my prayer
be granted

— —

heart ache

        break

i come

     to ask

for my

     good

29

I am busy building this wall

This wall goes up to the sky
I lose sight in its shadow

I plaster it with sand
All the care I take

I lose sight
of my being

--

                            he

                 who i enclose

         with my name

            weeps

in this dungeon

30

I came alone

Who follows me?

— —

          i move

          to avoid

          his presence

          he adds

          his loud

          voice to mine

he is

my own

little self

          shame

31

Prisoner
who bound you?

My master   in my own
treasure house

Prisoner
who forged this chain?

I

—-

    night

    and day

    i work

    at this chain

    unbreakable

32

They hold me secure
who love me

But love
is free

Love waits
for my love

——

i don't

call

you

keep

you

in my heart

      still

      love waits

33

They took their seat
in a corner   meek

In the night they break
into my shrine

—–

                                        they

snatch

   offerings

   from the altar

34

Let only that little bit be left of my will
where I feel you on every side

Let only that little bit be left of me
where I never hide

Let only that little of my fetters be left
that is the fetter of love

——

i

name

you

my all

come

to you

in

everything

35

Into freedom let my country awake

——

may

        the mind

   be

   without fear

      knowledge

   free

      world

   not broken

words come from truth

      reason not

lose   its way

      mind

        be led

           to ever-widening

             thought and action

36

My prayer   strike
at the penury in my heart

Give me the strength
to surrender my strength

with love

——

strike

strike

      make

            my love

fruitful

37

Sing of Life

I thought the path
was closed   provisions

exhausted   Time
to take shelter

in obscurity   But when
old words die new

melodies break forth
Old tracks are lost

new country is revealed

--

on

the tongue

in

the heart

wonder

38

The storm still seeks
its end in peace

when it strikes
against peace

—-—

night

hides

in its gloom

      my cry

            i want

            only

            you

39

When the heart is hard
come with a shower

When grace is lost
come with song

When work raises its din
come with peace

When my heart crouches
come with light & thunder

— —

lord

of silence

                    break

           open

the door

40

Rain has held
back in my heart   Horizon
is naked

Send storm   dark
with death   with lashes
of lightning

But call back
this silent heat burning
the heart with despair

Cloud of grace
bend low
from above

——

startle

                the sky

                    from

end

                              to end

41

My lover hides
in shadows   I wait   I spread

my offerings   Passers-by take
my flowers   My basket is empty

Morning is past   and noon   Like
a beggar I sit   drawing my skirt over my face

 I dream of sudden splendour   Lights blaze   Raise
me   a beggar girl   like a creeper in a summer breeze

Time glides on with shouts and
glamour   You stand silent behind

them all
I wait

--

raise

    me

        from the dust

42

We sail on our pilgrimage
to no country
to no end

In that shoreless ocean
my songs swell
free as waves   free

In fading light
seabirds fly
to their nests

—–

when

will

      the boat

           (last glimmer

           of sunset)

vanish

           into the night?

43

Enter my heart unbidden
even unknown to me

The steps I heard
in my room are

the same that echo
from star to star

——

the day

i did not

keep myself

in readiness

for you

44

Delight   to watch
shadows chase light and
rain

Tidings from unknown
skies speed along the road
The breeze is sweet

I know a sudden
happy moment
will arrive

Meanwhile I sing alone
Meanwhile the air fills
with perfume

--

my heart

   is glad

45

Have you heard his silent step?
He comes   comes   comes

Every moment   every age
every day   every night

he comes   comes   comes

In the fragrant days
he comes   comes   comes

In rainy gloom
he comes   comes   comes

In sorrow after sorrow
his steps press on my heart

The touch of his feet
makes my joy

shine

—-

he

                comes   comes   comes

through the forest

on thundering clouds

                          gold

46

From what distant time
do you come to meet me?

Today stirs joy
through my heart

The time has come

I feel a faint smell
of sweet presence

- -

your

       footsteps

             have been heard

i feel

         tremulous

47

Leave the way open for him

If his steps do
not wake me
let me sleep

My eyes will open
when he stands before me
like a dream emerging

from darkness   as
the first of all light
Let my return

to myself
be my return
to him

——

the first

    of all forms

the first

    thrill

48

Morning   Sea of silence
Ripples of bird songs

Gold scatter through clouds
Sun rises   Doves coo

Withered leaves whirl in noon
Dream in the shadow of the banyan tree

My companions vanish
Sun-embroidered green spreads

over my heart   I forgot for what
I had travelled   I surrender

When I woke I saw your smile   How
had I feared the path?

——

quicken pace more and more

     as time

          speeds by

i give

myself up

       for lost

          forget

for what

    i had travelled

49

You came
and stood by my door
I was singing

You came
and stood by my door
with a flower for a prize

You came
and stopped at my door

––

one strain

mingles

with the great music

my

      song

            struck your love

50

I wish I had the heart
to give my all

--

wait

for alms

      to be given

unasked

51

Distant thunder   Earth
shakes   walls rock   Wake

The king has come
but where are the lights?

Someone says *'Greet
him with empty hands'*   Let

conch shells sound   Darkness shudders
with lightning

--

                    lead him

into your room

bare

                    bring out

the tattered

mat

                    spread it

I thought I should ask
for the rose wreath on your neck

You depart   I find
on the bed a petal   I find

your sword heavy as a bolt
of thunder   No place to hide

it   This honour of pain   this
gift of yours   You left death

for my companion   I shall
crown him with my life   Your

sword is with me to cut my bonds
No fear for me

—-

i search

       in the dawn

young light

           spreads

      itself

on the bed

53

Beauty
Decked with stars   myriad-coloured jewels

More beautiful your sword   its curve
of lightning like outspread wings

It quivers
like the last response to life

Terrible to think of

——

       shine

like the flame

    burning

      with one

         fierce

flash

I asked nothing
Silent   The shadow

of a tree aslant

Women go home
with earthen pitchers full

I linger
Hear no steps   *'I am thirsty'*

I start   pour
water from my jar on your joined

palms   Leaves rustle   cuckoo
sings   perfume of babla flowers

from the bend   I stand
speechless with shame   What

have I done for you
to keep me in rememberance?

----

i sit

          and think

                    and think

55

Languor on heart
Slumber on eyes

The flower rises
among thorns   Wake

In the country of solitude
my friend   all alone   Wake

Sky pants with heat
Burning sand spreads its mantle

Is there joy in your heart?
The road breaks out in music

——

                    at the end

           of the stony

        path

solitude

56

Joy in me is full
Where would love be
if I were not?

Take me as partner
of all
this wealth

In my heart   delight

Decked in beauty
love loses itself
in love

––

you

come

to me

57

World-filling light
Eye-kissing light
Heart-sweeting light

Light dances
Light strikes
The sky opens

Wind runs wild
Laughter passes over
earth

Butterflies spread sails
                    on the sea of light

Jasmines & lilies surge
                    on waves of light

Light shatters gold on cloud
                    & scatters gems

Heaven's river has drowned
                        its banks

— —

my darling

      at the centre

of my life

                my darling

        gladness

    without

measure

58

Let all joy mingle

Joy
that makes earth flow
in grass

sets life and death
dancing

that throws
everything it has on the dust

that knows not a word

— —

in

my last

song

joy

sits still

on the open

red lotus

of pain

59

This is nothing
but love

This light   these
clouds   this breeze

on my forehead   Light floods
my eyes   bends

from above   looks
down on my eyes

this

is

your message

60

On the seashore of endless
worlds children meet

They build houses with sand   with
withered leaves weave boats

Children know
not how to swim   cast nets

The sea plays with children
Pale the smile of the beach

Tempests roam pathless sky   Ships wreck
in trackless water   Death is

On the seashore of endless
worlds is a meeting of children

--

sky

is motionless

restless

water

Sleep on baby's eyes
    know where it comes from?

Shadows of forests
    lit with glow worms

Sleep on baby's lips
    where was it born?

A beam of crescent moon
    touched an autumn cloud

Freshness on baby's limbs
    where was it hidden?

When the mother was a girl
    it pervaded her heart

--

      the dream

           of a dew-washed

morning

62

When I bring you toys
I understand why
          the play of colours
      flowers are in tints

When I sing to make you dance
I know why
          there is music in leaves
      waves send their voices
          to listening earth

When I bring sweet things
I know why
          there is honey in flowers
      fruits fill with sweet juice

When I kiss your face
I know what
          pleasure streams
      from the sky and
          the delight summer breeze
      brings to my body

— —

i kiss

     your face

         i kiss

            your face

63

Bring the distant near

I am unease
when I leave my shelter

In birth and death   in
this world or in others   wherever

companion of my life
link joy
to the unfamiliar

Grant
that I never
lose touch of the one
in many

— —

                alien

                is none

                no door

                is shut

may i

never

lose

bliss

64

On the river
among tall grass I ask   'Where
do you go shading your lamp? My
house is dark'
'*I float my lamp on a stream'*
I watch her lamp drift in the tide

In the silence
of the night I ask   '*Your lights are*
lit   Where do you go with your lamp?'
'*I dedicate my lamp to the sky'*
I watch light burning in the void

In moonless midnight I ask   '*What*
is your quest?'
'*I bought my lamp to join*
the carnival of lamps'
I watch her lamp lost among lights

——

look

at my face

      through the dusk

65

Listen
to eternal harmony

The world weaves words
in my mind

Joy adds music

—‑

        this overflowing

        cup

    of my

life

love

    feel

    your sweetness

in me

66

She remains
in my being   in
twilight   gleams
and glimpses   she
never opened her veil

She will be my last
gift   folded in song
Words have failed
to win her   I roam
keeping her in my heart

She reigns alone
apart   in loneliness
waiting recognition

— —

my last

gift   my final

song

67

You are
the sky
the nest as well

Comes the morning
with golden beauty

Comes the evening
through trackless paths
carrying peace

There
where spreads sky
reigns radiance

There is no day or night
no form or colour
never a word

——

o

beautiful

68

Sunbeam stands
at my door to carry
back clouds of tears and songs

Wrapping that mantle   turn
it into shapes and colour it

It is fleeting   tender and dark
Love it

It may cover awful
white light with its shadow

——

arms

           outstretched

        star

   and

shadow

69

The same stream of life that runs
through my veins runs through the world

The same life that shoots
through dust in blades of grass and
breaks into leaves and flowers

The same life is rocked
in the ocean-cradle
of birth and death

My limbs are made glorious
by its touch
My pride is the life-throb
dancing

—-

the same life

the same life

the same life

in my blood

70

Be glad with gladness   Be
lost and broken in fearful joy

All things rush on   rush on

Keeping step with that music
seasons dance   and pass

Perfumes pour

Joy scatters and gives up and dies
every moment

— —

is

it

beyond

you?

I make much of myself
Such is maya   Self

-separation
has taken body in me

Song echoes through
the sky   waves rise and
sink   dreams break and form

The screen is painted
with figures   Behind it is woven
mysteries   curves cast

away barren straightness   The pageant
has overspread the sky   the air is vibrant

Ages pass

——

                in me

is your defeat

He
the innermost one awakens
my being with his touch

He
puts enchantment
on eyes   plays on
my heart

He
weaves the web
of maya
in gold and silver
blue and green

His feet
at whose touch
I forget myself

He
moves in rapture

— —

deep

        hidden

                cadence

of pleasure

and pain

73

Deliverance is not for me in renunciation

I feel freedom
in bonds

Pour for me wine   fill this earthen
jar to the brim

My world will light its hundred
lamps and place them before the altar

I will never shut the doors of my senses
My illusions will burn into illumination

——

desires

      ripen

         into fruits

               of love

<h1 style="text-align:center">74</h1>

Shadow is on the earth
Sad music of water calls
into the dusk

In the lonely lane
the wind is up   Ripples
are rampant in the river

I know
not if I come
back home

— —

at

      the fording

         in a boat

           an unknown man

plays on his lute

75

Gifts to us mortals
fulfil our needs and
run back   undiminished

Worship does not
impoverish the world

⸺

from the words

of a poet

men take

meanings

      their last

         meaning

            points

               to you

Day after day with folded
hands I stand   face to face

Under your great sky in
silence I stand   face to face

In this world tumultuous with
struggle   I stand   face to face

When my work be done
shall I stand face to face

— —

in solitude

speechless

before you

I stand apart
and bow   In pleasure and

in pain I stand
not by the side of men

I shrink to give up
my life and

do not plunge
into the great waters

——

i do not know

                you

                        as my own

            clasp

        my heart

i share

my all

with you

When creation was new
stars shone in their first
splendour   The gods sang

One cried   *'Somewhere
there's a break   One
star is lost'*   Their harp snapped

The search is unceasing
Crying the world has
lost its one joy

In deep silence the stars
whisper   *'Unbroken
perfection is over all'*

--

in

      the sky

            in deepest night

        stars

smile

If it is not
my potion to meet in this life
let me not forget for a moment

this sorrow in my dreams and my wakeful hours

In the market
my hands grow full
with profit   Let
me feel I have gained nothing   Let
me not forget

this sorrow in my dreams and wakeful hours

When I spread
my bed in the dust
let me feel the long journey is still before me
Let me not forget   Let me carry

this sorrow in my dreams and wakeful hours

When my rooms are decked out
and laughter is loud
let me not forget this sorrow

--

carry the pangs

carry the pangs

tired and panting

carry the pangs

80

I am like a remnant
of a cloud in autumn
roaming
in the sky

Make me one
with light

Take this fleeting
emptiness   paint it
gild it   float it on the wind
Spread it

When it be your wish
to end this play
I shall melt in the dark or
be the morning transparent

——

I   count   the   months   and   years   separated   from   you

81

I grieve over lost time
But it is never lost   Take

every moment of my life
Hidden in the heart of things

seeds sprout   buds blossom   ripening
flowers fruit

I was sleeping and imagined
work had ceased   In the morning

I found my garden
full of wonders

——

i

woke

82

Time is endless
Know how to wait

Centuries follow
each other perfecting
a wild flower

Time   I give it to every
man who claims it
The altar is empty

At the end I find
yet there is time

——

no

      time

to lose

we are

      too poor

         to be

           late

83

Mother
I shall weave
a chain of tears

The stars
have wrought anklets
of light

Wealth and fame come   But
my sorrow is absolute
I bring it as offering

Reward me with grace

pearls

The pang
of separation spreads
gives birth to shapes
in the sky

This sorrow gazes
in silence from star
to star   becomes lyric
among rustling leaves

This pain deepens
into love and desire   this
melts and flows
through the poet's heart

--

                    infinite

sky

                separation

becomes lyric

        in rainy darkness

        this is it

and song

85

The warriors came out of their master's hall   Where
had they hidden their powers   armour   arms?

They looked poor and helpless
Arrows showered on them

The warriors marched back
Where did they hide their powers?

They left the fruits of their life
behind
           on their march to their master's hall

——

drop

sword

bow

arrow

                    peace

          on foreheads

86

Death is at my door

The night is dark
My heart is fearful

Yet I bow to him   I place
at his feet my heart

He will go back   leaving
a shadow on my morning

My self will remain
as my last offering

——

cross

                    the unknown

sea

I search for her   Find her
not   My house is small
What has gone can
never be regained

I stand under the golden
canopy of sky   lift my eyes

I have come
to the brink of eternity
from which nothing
can vanish

The deepest fullness

Let me feel
the allness
of the universe

--

desperate

　　　hope

　　　　　in infinity

dip

my emptied

life

　　　into that ocean

88

Deity of the ruined temple
the vina sings no more
Spring breeze brings
tidings of flowers that are offered
no more

Your worshipper wanders
with hunger in his heart   Festival
day comes in silence   Lamp unlit

New images are built and carried
to the holy stream

The deity of the ruined temple remains
unworshipped in deathless
neglect

— —

        your worshipper of old

     longing

   still refused

fires   shadows

gloom   dust

oblivion

89

No more loud
words for me
I deal in whispers

Men hasten
to the market
I leave

Let flowers come
out of my garden
though it is not time

Empty days
draw my heart
to what inconsequence?

--

murmurings

        of song

this sudden

      call

90

On the day death
knocks I will never
let him go with empty

hands   Sweet vintage
of my days and nights
earnings and gleanings

I will place
before him

--

what

will

you offer?

    the full

        vessel

           of my life

              at the close

    of my days

91

Last fulfilment of life   Death
come to me   I have kept watch

All that I am   have   hope   all
my love flows towards you

in secrecy   The garland
is ready for the bridegroom

——

the bride

shall leave

her home

in

the solitude

of night

92

My sight shall be lost
Life will draw the curtain
over my eyes

Yet stars will watch and
morning rise and
hours heave like sea waves

When I think of this end
the barrier of moments breaks
I see the world

with its careless treasures   Rare
is its lowliest seat   rare
its meanest life

Things I longed for and
things I got   let them pass   Let
me possess the things I spurned

— —

i see

by the light

of death

93

I have my leave
I bow to you all

I give back
the keys to my door

I received
more than I could give

The day has dawned
The lamp is out

Summons
I am ready for my journey

— —

farewell

94

At parting   the sky
is flushed with dawn

I start my journey with
empty hands   expectant heart

I put on my wedding garland   Though
there are dangers I have no fear

Evening star will come out
when my journey is done

— —

wish me

    luck

        my path

          lies

            beautiful

What power made me open
into this vast mystery like a bud
in a forest at midnight?

I am no stranger
in this world   The inscrutable
has taken me in its arms

In death the same
unknown will appear
as known

Because I love life
I shall love death as well

--

i

      was not

        aware

  when

  i crossed

the threshold

of life

96

When I go
let this be my parting word

what I have seen
is unsurpassable

Am I blessed

In infinite forms
I have sighted him

that is formless

--

i

have tasted

hidden honey

my body

thrills

with his touch

who is

beyond

touch

97

My life was boisterous
I never cared to know
the meaning of songs

Now playtime is over

The world stands
in awe with all
its silent stars

— —

call me

      from sleep

              lead me

running

      from glade

to   glade

98

It is never in my power
to escape unconquered

I know my life will burst
in pain   Stone will melt

The hundred-petalled lotus will
not remain closed   the secret

of its honey will be bared
From the sky an eye

shall summon me   Nothing
will be left   Nothing

Utter death

— —

i

deck

you

      with garlands

of my

defeat

99

Vain is struggle   Put
up with your defeat heart
My lamps are blown out

But I wait
in the dark   Whatever is
your pleasure   come

—–

i know

the time

has come

100

I dive into the ocean
of forms to gain the pearl
of the formless

No more sailing
with my weather-beaten boat

I am eager to die
into the deathless   into
the music
of toneless strings

I take this harp   tune
it to the notes of
forever

--

in

       the fathomless

abyss

    swells

          music

i shall

take

this harp

of my life

lay silence

at

silence

101

I have sought you

with my songs   With them
I searched and touched my world

They showed me secret paths   stars
on the horizon of my heart

To what gate have they
brought me at the end?

— —

with

      my songs

            i feel about

                  searching, touching

                            guide

                me to

                    the mysteries

102

I boasted I had known you

They see your pictures
in works of mine   They ask
'Who is he?'

'I cannot tell'
They go away in scorn   And
you sit there smiling

I put my tales of you
into songs   They ask
'Tell me your meanings'

'Who knows?'
They go away in scorn   And
you sit there smiling

                                                        --

                                                       i

                                                    put you

into lasting

                                                  songs

103

In one salutation
let my senses spread out and touch
this world

Let my mind bend in one salutation
Let my songs gather and flow to a sea of silence
in one salutation

Like a flock of homesick cranes flying back
let my life take to its eternal home
in one salutation

—

like a rain-cloud

hung

low

shed

showers

       let my life

            take its voyage

                to you

RABINDRANATH TAGORE'S
GITANJALI

*A Collection of Prose Translations
made by the Author from the Original Bengali
with an Introduction by W.B. Yeats*

1

THOU hast made me endless, such is thy pleasure. This frail
vessel thou emptiest again and again, and fillest it ever with
fresh life.

This little flute of a reed thou hast carried over hills and dales, and
hast breathed through it melodies eternally new.

At the immortal touch of thy hands my little heart loses its limits
in joy and gives birth to utterance ineffable.

Thy infinite gifts come to me only on these very small hands of
mine. Ages pass, and still thou pourest, and still there is room
to fill.

2

WHEN thou commandest me to sing it seems that my heart
would break with pride; and I look to thy face, and tears come to
my eyes.

All that is harsh and dissonant in my life melts into one sweet
harmony —and my adoration spreads wings like a glad bird on its
flight across the sea.

I know thou takest pleasure in my singing. I know that only as a
singer I come before thy presence.

I touch by the edge of the far spreading wing of my song thy feet
which I could never aspire to reach.

Drunk with the joy of singing I forget myself and call thee friend
who art my lord.

3

I KNOW not how thou singest, my master! I ever listen in silent
amazement.

The light of thy music illumines the world. The life breath of thy
music runs from sky to sky. The holy stream of thy music breaks

through all stony obstacles and rushes on. My heart longs to join
in thy song, but vainly struggles for a voice. I would speak, but
speech breaks not into song, and I cry out baffled. Ah, thou hast
made my heart captive in the endless meshes of thy music,
my master!

4

LIFE of my life, I shall ever try to keep my body pure, knowing
that thy living touch is upon all my limbs.

I shall ever try to keep all untruths out from my thoughts,
knowing that thou art that truth which has kindled the light of
reason in my mind.

I shall ever try to drive all evils away from my heart and keep
my love in flower, knowing that thou hast thy seat in the inmost
shrine of my heart.

And it shall be my endeavour to reveal thee in my actions,
knowing it is thy power gives me strength to act.

5

I ASK for a moment's indulgence to sit by thy side. The works that
I have in hand I will finish afterwards.

Away from the sight of thy face my heart knows no rest nor
respite, and my work becomes an endless toil in a shoreless sea
of toil.

To-day the summer has come at my window with its sighs and
murmurs; and the bees are plying their minstrelsy at the court of
the flowering grove.

Now it is time to sit quiet, face to face with thee, and to sing
dedication of life in this silent and overflowing leisure.

6

PLUCK this little flower and take it, delay not! I fear lest it droop and drop into the dust.

It may not find a place in thy garland, but honour it with a touch of pain from thy hand and pluck it. I fear lest the day end before I am aware, and the time of offering go by.

Though its colour be not deep and its smell be faint, use this flower in thy service and pluck it while there is time.

7

MY song has put off her adornments.

She has no pride of dress and decoration. Ornaments would mar our union; they would come between thee and me; their jingling would drown thy whispers.

My poet's vanity dies in shame before thy sight. O master poet, I have sat down at thy feet. Only let me make my life simple and straight, like a flute of reed for thee to fill with music.

8

THE child who is decked with prince's robes and who has jewelled chains round his neck loses all pleasure in his play; his dress hampers him at every step.

In fear that it may be frayed, or stained with dust he keeps himself from the world, and is afraid even to move.

Mother, it is no gain, thy bondage of finery, if it keep one shut off from the healthful dust of the earth, if it rob one of the right of entrance to the great fair of common human life.

9

O FOOL, to try to carry thyself upon thy own shoulders! O beggar, to come to beg at thy own door!

Leave all thy burdens on his hands who can bear all, and never look behind in regret.

Thy desire at once puts out the light from the lamp it touches with its breath.

It is unholy — take not thy gifts through its unclean hands. Accept only what is offered by sacred love.

10

HERE is thy footstool and there rest thy feet where live the poorest, and lowliest, and lost.

When I try to bow to thee, my obeisance cannot reach down to the depth where thy feet rest among the poorest, and lowliest, and lost.

Pride can never approach to where thou walkest in the clothes of the humble among the poorest, and lowliest, and lost.

My heart can never find its way to where thou keepest company with the companionless among the poorest, the lowliest, and the lost.

11

LEAVE this chanting and singing and telling of beads! Whom dost thou worship in this lonely dark corner of a temple with doors all shut? Open thine eyes and see thy God is not before thee!

He is there where the tiller is tilling the hard ground and where the path-maker is breaking stones. He is with them in sun and in shower, and his garment is covered with dust. Put off thy holy mantle and even like him come down on the dusty soil!

Deliverance? Where is this deliverance to be found? Our master himself has joyfully taken upon him the bonds of creation; he is bound with us all for ever.

Come out of thy meditations and leave aside thy flowers and incense! What harm is there if thy clothes become tattered and stained? Meet him and stand by him in toil and in sweat of thy brow.

12

THE time that my journey takes is long and the way of it long.

I came out on the chariot of the first gleam of light, and pursued my voyage through the wildernesses of worlds leaving my track on many a star and planet.

It is the most distant course that comes nearest to thyself, and that training is the most intricate which leads to the utter simplicity of a tune.

The traveller has to knock at every alien door to come to his own, and one has to wander through all the outer worlds to reach the innermost shrine at the end.

My eyes strayed far and wide before I shut them and said "Here art thou!"

The question and the cry "Oh, where?" melt into tears of a thousand streams and deluge the world with the flood of the assurance "I am!"

13

THE song that I came to sing remains unsung to this day.

I have spent my days in stringing and in unstringing my instrument.

The time has not come true, the words have not been rightly set; only there is the agony of wishing in my heart.

The blossom has not opened; only the wind is sighing by.

I have not seen his face, nor have I listened to his voice; only I have heard his gentle footsteps from the road before my house.

The livelong day has passed in spreading his seat on the floor; but the lamp has not been lit and I cannot ask him into my house.

I live in the hope of meeting with him; but this meeting is not yet.

14

MY desires are many and my cry is pitiful, but ever didst thou save me by hard refusals; and this strong mercy has been wrought into my life through and through.

Day by day thou art making me worthy of the simple, great gifts that thou gavest to me unasked — this sky and the light, this body and the life and the mind — saving me from perils of overmuch desire.

There are times when I languidly linger and times when I awaken and hurry in search of my goal; but cruelly thou hidest thyself from before me.

Day by day thou art making me worthy of thy full acceptance by refusing me ever and anon, saving me from perils of weak, uncertain desire.

15

I AM here to sing thee songs. In this hall of thine I have a corner seat.

In thy world I have no work to do; my useless life can only break out in tunes without a purpose.

When the hour strikes for thy silent worship at dark temple of midnight, command me, my master, to stand before thee to sing.

When in the morning air the golden harp is tuned, honour me, commanding my presence.

16

I HAVE had my invitation to this world's festival, and thus my life has been blessed. My eyes have seen and my ears have heard.

It was my part at this feast to play upon my instrument, and I have done all I could.

Now, I ask, has the time come at last when I may go in and see thy face and offer thee my silent salutation?

17

I AM only waiting for love to give myself up at last into his hands. That is why it is so late and why I have been guilty of such omissions.

They come with their laws and their codes to bind me fast; but I evade them ever, for I am only waiting for love to give myself up at last into his hands.

People blame me and call me heedless; I doubt not they are right in their blame.

The market day is over and work is all done for the busy. Those who came to call me in vain have gone back in anger. I am only waiting for love to give myself up at last into his hands.

18

CLOUDS heap upon clouds and it darkens. Ah, love, why dost thou let me wait outside at the door all alone?

In the busy moments of the noontide work I am with the crowd, but on this dark lonely day it is only for thee that I hope.

If thou showest me not thy face, if thou leavest me wholly aside, I know not how I am to pass these long, rainy hours.

I keep gazing on the far away gloom of the sky, and my heart wanders wailing with the restless wind.

19

IF thou speakest not I will fill my heart with thy silence and endure it. I will keep still and wait like the night with starry vigil and its head bent low with patience.

The morning will surely come, the darkness will vanish, and thy voice pour down in golden streams breaking through the sky.

Then thy words will take wing in songs from every one of my birds' nests, and thy melodies will break forth in flowers in all my forest groves.

20

ON the day when the lotus bloomed, alas, my mind was straying, and I knew it not. My basket was empty and the flower remained unheeded.

Only now and again a sadness fell upon me, and I started up from my dream and felt a sweet trace of a strange fragrance in the south wind.

That vague sweetness made my heart ache with longing and it seemed to me that it was the eager breath of the summer seeking for its completion.

I knew not then that it was so near, that it was mine, and that this perfect sweetness had blossomed in the depth of my own heart.

21

I MUST launch out my boat. The languid hours pass by on the shore — Alas for me!

The spring has done its flowering and taken leave. And now with the burden of faded futile flowers I wait and linger.

The waves have become clamorous, and upon the bank in the shady lane the yellow leaves flutter and fall.

What emptiness do you gaze upon!

Do you not feel a thrill passing through the air with the notes of the far away song floating from the other shore?

22

IN the deep shadows of the rainy July, with secret steps, thou walkest, silent as night, eluding all watchers.

To-day the morning has closed its eyes, heedless of the insistent calls of the loud east wind, and a thick veil has been drawn over the ever-wakeful blue sky.

The woodlands have hushed their songs, and doors are all shut at every house. Thou art the solitary wayfarer in this deserted street. Oh my only friend, my best beloved, the gates are open in my house — do not pass by like a dream.

23

ART thou abroad on this stormy night on the journey of love, my friend? The sky groans like one in despair.

I have no sleep to-night. Ever and again I open my door and look out on the darkness, my friend!

I can see nothing before me. I wonder where lies thy path!

By what dim shore of the ink-black river, by what far edge of the frowning forest, through what mazy depth of gloom art thou threading thy course to come to me, my friend?

24

IF the day is done, if birds sing no more, if the wind has flagged tired, then draw the veil of darkness thick upon me, even as thou hast wrapt the earth with the coverlet of sleep and tenderly closed the petals of the drooping lotus at dusk.

From the traveller, whose sack of provisions is empty before the voyage is ended, whose garment is torn and dust-laden, whose strength is exhausted, remove shame and poverty, and renew his life like a flower under the cover of thy kindly night.

25

IN the night of weariness let me give myself up to sleep without struggle, resting my trust upon thee.

Let me not force my flagging spirit into a poor preparation for thy worship.

It is thou who drawest the veil of night upon the tired eyes of the day to renew its sight in a fresher gladness of awakening.

26

HE came and sat by my side but I woke not. What a cursed sleep it was, O miserable me!

He came when the night was still; he had his harp in his hands, and my dreams became resonant with its melodies.

Alas, why are my nights all thus lost? Ah, why do I ever miss his sight whose breath touches my sleep?

27

LIGHT, oh where is the light? Kindle it with the burning fire of desire!

There is the lamp but never a flicker of a flame, — is such thy fate, my   heart! Ah, death

were better by far for thee!

Misery knocks at thy door, and her message is that thy lord is wakeful, and he calls thee to thy love-tryst through the darkness of night.

The sky is overcast with clouds and the rain is ceaseless. I know not what this is that stirs in me, — I know not its meaning.

A moment's flash of lightning drags down a deeper gloom on my sight, and my heart gropes for the path to where the music of the night calls me.

Light, oh where is the light! Kindle it with the burning fire of desire! It thunders and the wind rushes screaming through the void. The night is black as a black stone. Let not the hours pass by in the dark. Kindle the lamp of love with thy life.

28

OBSTINATE are the trammels, but my heart aches when I try to break them.

Freedom is all I want, but to hope for it I feel ashamed.

I am certain that priceless wealth is in thee, and that thou art my best friend, but I have not the heart to sweep away the tinsel that fills my room.

The shroud that covers me is a shroud of dust and death; I hate it, yet hug it in love. My debts are large, my failures great, my shame secret and heavy; yet when I come to ask for my good, I quake in fear lest my prayer be granted.

29

HE whom I enclose with my name is weeping in this dungeon. I am ever busy building this wall all around; and as this wall goes up into the sky day by day I lose sight of my true being in its dark shadow.

I take pride in this great wall, and I plaster it with dust and sand lest a least hole should be left in this name; and for all the care I take I lose sight of my true being.

30

I CAME out alone on my way to my tryst. But who is this that follows me in the silent dark?

I move aside to avoid his presence but I escape him not.

He makes the dust rise from the earth with his swagger; he adds his loud voice to every word that I utter.

He is my own little self, my lord, he knows no shame; but I am ashamed to come to thy door in his company.

31

"PRISONER, tell me, who was it that bound you?"

"It was my master," said the prisoner.

"I thought I could outdo everybody in the world in wealth and power, and I amassed in my own treasure-house the money due to my king. When sleep overcame me I lay upon the bed that was for my lord, and on waking up I found I was a prisoner in my own treasure-house."

"Prisoner, tell me who was it that wrought this unbreakable chain?"

"It was I," said the prisoner, "who forged this chain very carefully. I thought my invincible power would hold the world captive leaving me in a freedom undisturbed. Thus night and day I worked at the chain with huge fires and cruel hard strokes. When at last the work was done and the links were complete and unbreakable, I found that it held me in its grip."

32

BY all means they try to hold me secure who love me in this world. But it is otherwise with thy love which is greater than theirs, and thou keepest me free.

Lest I forget them they never venture to leave me alone. But day passes by after day and thou art not seen.

If I call not thee in my prayers, if I keep not thee in my heart, thy love for me still waits for my love.

33

WHEN it was day they came into my house and said, "We shall only take the smallest room here."

They said, "We shall help you in the worship of your God and humbly accept only our own share of his grace"; and then they took their seat in a corner and they sat quiet and meek.

But in the darkness of night I find they break into my sacred shrine, strong and turbulent, and snatch with unholy greed the offerings from God's altar.

34

LET only that little be left of me whereby I may name thee my all.

Let only that little be left of my will whereby I may feel thee on everyside, and come to thee in everything, and offer to thee my love every moment.

Let only that little be left of me whereby I may never hide thee.

Let only that little of my fetters be left whereby I am bound with thy will, and thy purpose is carried out in my life — and that is the fetter of thy love.

35

WHERE the mind is without fear and the head is held high;

Where knowledge is free;

Where the world has not been broken up into fragments by narrow domestic walls;

Where words come out from the depth of truth;

Where tireless striving stretches its arms towards perfection;

Where the clear stream of reason has not lost its way into the dreary desert sand of dead habit;

Where the mind is led forward by thee into ever-widening thought and action —

Into that heaven of freedom, my Father, let my country awake.

36

THIS is my prayer to thee, my lord — strike, strike at the root of penury in my heart.

Give me the strength lightly to bear my joys and sorrows.

Give me the strength to make my love fruitful in service.

Give me the strength never to disown the poor or bend my knees before insolent might.

Give me the strength to raise my mind high above daily trifles.

And give me the strength to surrender my strength to thy will with love.

37

I THOUGHT that my voyage had come to its end at the last limit of my power, — that the path before me was closed, that provisions were exhausted and the time come to take shelter in a silent obscurity.

But I find that thy will knows no end in me. And when old words die out on the tongue, new melodies break forth from the heart; and where the old tracks are lost, new country is revealed with its wonders.

38

THAT I want thee, only thee — let my heart repeat without end. All desires that distract me, day and night, are false and empty to the core.

As the night keeps hidden in its gloom the petition for light, even thus in the depth of my unconsciousness rings the cry — I want thee, only thee.

As the storm still seeks its end in peace when it strikes against peace with all its might, even thus my rebellion strikes against thy love and still its cry is — I want thee, only thee.

39

WHEN the heart is hard and parched up, come upon me with a shower of mercy.

When grace is lost from life, come with a burst of song.

When tumultuous work raises its din on all sides shutting me out from beyond, come to me, my lord of silence, with thy peace and rest.

When my beggarly heart sits crouched, shut up in a corner, break open the door, my king, and come with the ceremony of a king.

When desire blinds the mind with delusion and dust, thou holy one, thou wakeful, come with thy light and thy thunder.

40

THE rain has held back for days and days, my God, in my arid heart. The horizon is fiercely naked — not the thinnest cover of a soft cloud, not the vaguest hint of a distant cool shower.

Send thy angry storm, dark with death, if it is thy wish, and with lashes of lightning startle the sky from end to end.

But call back, my lord, call back this pervading silent heat, still and keen and cruel, burning the heart with dire despair.

Let the cloud of grace bend low from above like the tearful look of the mother on the day of the father's wrath.

41

WHERE dost thou stand behind them all, my lover, hiding thyself in the shadows? They push thee and pass thee by on the dusty road, taking thee for naught. I wait here weary hours spreading my offerings for thee, while passers by come and take my flowers, one by one, and my basket is nearly empty.

The morning time is past, and the noon. In the shade of evening my eyes are drowsy with sleep. Men going home glance at me and smile and fill me with shame. I sit like a beggar maid, drawing my skirt over my face, and when they ask me, what it is I want, I drop my eyes and answer them not.

Oh, how, indeed, could I tell them that for thee I wait, and that thou hast promised to come. How could I utter for shame that I keep for my dowry this poverty. Ah, I hug this pride in the secret of my heart.

I sit on the grass and gaze upon the sky and dream of the sudden splendour of thy coming — all the lights ablaze, golden pennons flying over thy car, and they at the roadside standing agape, when they see thee come down from thy seat to raise me from the dust, and set at thy side this ragged beggar girl a-tremble with shame and pride, like a creeper in a summer breeze.

But time glides on and still no sound of the wheels of thy chariot. Many a procession passes by with noise and shouts and glamour of glory. Is it only thou who wouldst stand in the shadow silent and behind them all? And only I who would wait and weep and wear out my heart in vain longing?

42

EARLY in the day it was whispered that we should sail in a boat, only thou and I, and never a soul in the world would know of this our pilgrimage to no country and to no end.

In that shoreless ocean, at thy silently listening smile my songs would swell in melodies, free as waves, free from all bondage of words.

Is the time not come yet? Are there works still to do? Lo, the evening has come down upon the shore and in the fading light the seabirds come flying to their nests.

Who knows when the chains will be off, and the boat, like the last glimmer of sunset, vanish into the night?

43

THE day was when I did not keep myself in readiness for thee; and entering my heart unbidden even as one of the common crowd, unknown to me, my king, thou didst press the signet of eternity upon many a fleeting moment of my life.

And to-day when by chance I light upon them and see thy signature, I find they have lain scattered in the dust mixed with the memory of joys and sorrows of my trivial days forgotten.

Thou didst not turn in contempt from my childish play among dust, and the steps that I heard in my playroom are the same that are echoing from star to star.

44

THIS is my delight, thus to wait and watch at the wayside where shadow chases light and the rain comes in the wake of the summer.

Messengers, with tidings from unknown skies, greet me and speed along the road. My heart is glad within, and the breath of the passing breeze is sweet.

From dawn till dusk I sit here before my door, and I know that of a sudden the happy moment will arrive when I shall see.

In the meanwhile I smile and I sing all alone. In the meanwhile the air is filling with the perfume of promise.

45

HAVE you not heard his silent, steps?

He comes, comes, ever comes.

Every moment and every age, every day and every night he comes, comes, ever comes.

Many a song have I sung in many a mood of mind, but all their notes have always proclaimed, "He comes, comes, ever comes."

In the fragrant days of sunny April through the forest path he comes, comes, ever comes.

In the rainy gloom of July nights on the thundering chariot of clouds he comes, comes, ever comes.

In sorrow after sorrow it is his steps that press upon my heart, and it is the golden touch of his feet that makes my joy to shine.

46

I KNOW not from what distant time thou art ever coming nearer to meet me. Thy sun and stars can never keep thee hidden from me for aye.

In many a morning and eve thy footsteps have been heard and thy messenger has come within my heart and called me in secret.

I know not why to-day my life is all astir, and a feeling of tremulous joy is passing through my heart.

It is as if the time were come to wind up my work, and I feel in the air a faint smell of thy sweet presence.

47

THE night is nearly spent waiting for him in vain. I fear lest in the morning he suddenly come to my door when I have fallen asleep wearied out. Oh friends, leave the way open to him — forbid him not.

If the sound of his steps does not wake me, do not try to rouse me, I pray. I wish not to be called from my sleep by the clamorous choir of birds, by the riot of wind at the festival of morning light. Let me sleep undisturbed even if my lord comes of a sudden to my door.

Ah, my sleep, precious sleep, which only waits for his touch to vanish.

Ah, my closed eyes that would open their lids to the light of his smile when he stands before me like a dream emerging from darkness of sleep.

Let him appear before my sight as the first of all lights and all forms. The first thrill of joy to my awakened soul let it come from his glance. And let my return to myself be immediate return to him.

48

THE morning sea of silence broke into ripples of bird songs; and the flowers were all merry by the roadside; and the wealth of gold was scattered through the rift of the clouds while we busily went on our way and paid no heed.

We sang no glad songs nor played; we went not to the village for barter; we spoke not a word nor smiled; we lingered not on the way. We quickened our pace more and more as the time sped by.

The sun rose to the mid sky and doves cooed in the shade. Withered leaves danced and whirled in the hot air of noon. The shepherd boy drowsed and dreamed in the shadow of the banyan tree, and I laid myself down by the water and stretched my tired limbs on the grass.

My companions laughed at me in scorn; they held their heads high and hurried on; they never looked back nor rested; they vanished in the distant blue haze. They crossed many meadows and hills, and passed through strange, far-away countries. All honour to you, heroic host of the interminable path! Mockery and reproach pricked me to rise, but found no response in me. I gave myself up for lost in the depth of a glad humiliation — in the shadow of a dim delight.

The repose of the sun-embroidered green gloom slowly spread over my heart. I forgot for what I had travelled, and I surrendered my mind without struggle to the maze of shadows and songs.

At last, when I woke from my slumber and opened my eyes, I saw thee standing by me, flooding my sleep with thy smile. How I had

feared that the path was long and wearisome, and the struggle to
reach thee was hard!

49

YOU came down from your throne and stood at my cottage door.

I was singing all alone in a corner, and the melody caught your ear.
You came down and stood at my cottage door.

Masters are many in your hall, and songs are sung there at all
hours. But the simple carol of this novice struck at your love. One
plaintive little strain mingled with the great music of the world,
and with a flower for a prize you came down and stopped at my
cottage door.

50

I HAD gone a-begging from door to door in the village path, when
thy golden chariot appeared in the distance like a gorgeous dream
and I wondered who was this King of all kings!

My hopes rose high and me thought my evil days were at an end,
and I stood waiting for alms to be given unasked and for wealth
scattered on all sides in the dust.

The chariot stopped where I stood. Thy glance fell on me and thou
earnest down with a smile. I felt that the luck of my life had come
at last. Then of a sudden thou didst hold out thy right hand and
say "What hast thou to give to me?"

Ah, what a kingly jest was it to open thy palm to a beggar to beg!
I was confused and stood undecided, and then from my wallet I
slowly took out the least little grain of corn and gave it to thee.

But how great my surprise when at the day's end I emptied my bag
on the floor to find a least little grain of gold among the poor heap.
I bitterly wept and wished that I had had the heart to give thee
my all.

51

THE night darkened. Our day's works had been done. We thought that the last guest had arrived for the night and the doors in the village were all shut. Only some said, The king was to come. We laughed and said "No, it cannot be!"

It seemed there were knocks at the door and we said it was nothing but the wind. We put out the lamps and lay down to sleep. Only some said, "It is the messenger!" We laughed and said "No, it must be the wind!"

There came a sound in the dead of the night. We sleepily thought it was the distant thunder. The earth shook, the walls rocked, and it troubled us in our sleep. Only some said, it was the sound of wheels. We said in a drowsy murmur, "No, it must be the rumbling of clouds!"

The night was still dark when the drum sounded. The voice came "Wake up! Delay not! "We pressed our hands on our hearts and shuddered with fear. Some said, "Lo, there is the king's flag!" We stood up on our feet and cried "There is no time for delay!"

The king has come but where are lights, where are wreaths? Where is the throne to seat him? Oh, shame! Oh utter shame! Where is the hall, the decorations? Some one has said, "Vain is this cry! Greet him with empty hands, lead him into thy rooms all bare!"

Open the doors, let the conch-shells be sounded! In the depth of the night has come the king of our dark, dreary house. The thunder roars in the sky. The darkness shudders with lightning. Bring out thy tattered piece of mat and spread it in the courtyard. With the storm has come of a sudden our king of the fearful night.

52

I THOUGHT I should ask of thee — but I dared not — the rose wreath thou hadst on thy neck. Thus I waited for the morning, when thou didst depart, to find a few fragments on the bed. And like a beggar I searched in the dawn only for a stray petal or two.

Ah me, what is it I find? What token left of thy love? It is no flower, no spices, no vase of perfumed water. It is thy mighty sword, flashing as a flame, heavy as a bolt of thunder. The young light of morning comes through the window and spreads itself upon thy bed. The morning bird twitters and asks, "Woman, what hast thou got?" No, it is no flower, nor spices, nor vase of perfumed water — it is thy dreadful sword.

I sit and muse in wonder, what gift is this of thine. I can find no place where to hide it. I am ashamed to wear it, frail as I am, and it hurts me when I press it to my bosom. Yet shall I bear in my heart this honour of the burden of pain, this gift of thine.

From now there shall be no fear left for me in this world, and thou shalt be victorious in all my strife. Thou hast left death for my companion and I shall crown him with my life. Thy sword is with me to cut asunder my bonds, and there shall be no fear left for me in the world.

From now I leave off all petty decorations. Lord of my heart, no more shall there be for me waiting and weeping in corners, no more coyness and sweetness of demeanour. Thou hast given me thy sword for adornment. No more doll's decorations for me!

53

BEAUTIFUL is thy wristlet, decked with stars and cunningly wrought in myriad-coloured jewels. But more beautiful to me thy sword with its curve of lightning like the outspread wings of the divine bird of Vishnu, perfectly poised in the angry red light of the sunset.

It quivers like the one last response of life in ecstasy of pain at the final stroke of death; it shines like the pure flame of being burning up earthly sense with one fierce flash.

Beautiful is thy wristlet, decked with starry gems; but thy sword, O lord of thunder, is wrought with uttermost beauty, terrible to behold or to think of.

54

I ASKED nothing from thee; I uttered not my name to thine ear.
When thou took'st thy leave I stood silent. I was alone by the well
where the shadow of the tree fell aslant, and the women had gone
home with their brown earthen pitchers full to the brim. They
called me and shouted, "Come with us, the morning is wearing on
to noon." But I languidly lingered awhile lost in the midst of vague
musings.

I heard not thy steps as thou camest. Thine eyes were sad when
they fell on me; thy voice was tired as thou spokest low — "Ah,
I am a thirsty traveller." I started up from my day-dreams and
poured water from my jar on thy joined palms. The leaves rustled
overhead; the cuckoo sang from the unseen dark, and perfume of
babla flowers came from the bend of the road.

I stood speechless with shame when my name thou didst ask.
Indeed, what had I done for thee to keep me in remembrance? But
the memory that I could give water to thee to allay thy thirst will
cling to my heart and enfold it in sweetness. The morning hour
is late, the bird sings in weary notes, neem leaves rustle overhead
and I sit and think and think.

55

LANGUOR is upon your heart and the slumber is still on your
eyes.

Has not the word come to you that the flower is reigning in
splendour among thorns? Wake, oh awaken! Let not the time pass
in vain!

At the end of the stony path, in the country of virgin solitude my
friend is sitting all alone. Deceive him not. Wake, oh awaken!

What if the sky pants and trembles with the heat of the midday
sun — what if the burning sand spreads its mantle of thirst —

Is there no joy in the deep of your heart? At every footfall of yours,
will not the harp of the road break out in sweet music of pain?

56

THUS it is that thy joy in me is so full. Thus it is that thou hast come down to me. O thou lord of all heavens, where would be thy love if I were not?

Thou hast taken me as thy partner of all this wealth. In my heart is the endless play of thy delight. In my life thy will is ever taking shape.

And for this, thou who art the King of kings hast decked thyself in beauty to captivate my heart. And for this thy love loses itself in the love of thy lover, and there art thou seen in the perfect union of two.

57

LIGHT, my light, the world-filling light, the eye-kissing light, heart-sweetening light!

Ah, the light dances, my darling, at the centre of my life; the light strikes, my darling, the chords of my love; the sky opens, the wind runs wild, laughter passes over the earth.

The butterflies spread their sails on the sea of light. Lilies and jasmines surge up on the crest of the waves of light.

The light is shattered into gold on every cloud, my darling, and it scatters gems in profusion.

Mirth spreads from leaf to leaf, my darling, and gladness without measure. The heaven's river has drowned its banks and the flood of joy is abroad.

58

LET all the strains of joy mingle in my last song — the joy that makes the earth flow over in the riotous excess of the grass, the joy that sets the twin brothers, life and death, dancing over the wide world, the joy that sweeps in with the tempest, shaking and waking all life with laughter, the joy that sits still with its tears on

the open red lotus of pain, and the joy that throws everything it
has upon the dust, and knows not a word.

59

YES, I know, this is nothing but thy love, O beloved of my heart
— this golden light that dances upon the leaves, these idle clouds
sailing across the sky, this passing breeze leaving its coolness upon
my forehead.

The morning light has flooded my eyes — this is thy message to
my heart. Thy face is bent from above, thy eyes look down on my
eyes, and my heart has touched thy feet.

60

ON the seashore of endless worlds children meet. The infinite
sky is motionless overhead and the restless water is boisterous.
On the seashore of endless worlds the children meet with shouts
and dances.

They build their houses with sand and they play with empty shells.
With withered leaves they weave their boats and smilingly float
them on the vast deep. Children have their play on the seashore
of worlds.

They know not how to swim, they know not how to cast nets.
Pearl fishers dive for pearls, merchants sail in their ships, while
children gather pebbles and scatter them again. They seek not for
hidden treasures, they know not how to cast nets.

The sea surges up with laughter and pale gleams the smile of the
sea beach. Death- dealing waves sing meaningless ballads to the
children, even like a mother while rocking her baby's cradle. The
sea plays with children, and pale gleams the smile of the sea beach.

On the seashore of endless worlds children meet. Tempest roams
in the pathless sky, ships get wrecked in the trackless water, death
is abroad and children play. On the seashore of endless worlds is
the great meeting of children.

61

THE sleep that flits on baby's eyes — does anybody know from where it comes? Yes, there is a rumour that it has its dwelling where, in the fairy village among shadows of the forest dimly lit with glow-worms, there hang two timid buds of enchantment. From there it comes to kiss baby's eyes.

The smile that flickers on baby's lips when he sleeps — does anybody know where it was born? Yes, there is a rumour that a young pale beam of a crescent moon touched the edge of a vanishing autumn cloud, and there the smile was first born in the dream of a dew-washed morning — the smile that flickers on baby's lips when he sleeps.

The sweet, soft freshness that blooms on baby's limbs — does anybody know where it was hidden so long? Yes, when the mother was a young girl it lay pervading her heart in tender and silent mystery of love — the sweet, soft freshness that has bloomed on baby's limbs.

62

WHEN I bring to you coloured toys, my child, I understand why there is such a play of colours on clouds, on water, and why flowers are painted in tints — when I give coloured toys to you, my child.

When I sing to make you dance I truly know why there is music in leaves, and why waves send their chorus of voices to the heart of the listening earth — when I sing to make you dance.

When I bring sweet things to your greedy hands I know why there is honey in the cup of the flower and why fruits are secretly filled with sweet juice — when I bring sweet things to your greedy hands.

When I kiss your face to make you smile, my darling, I surely understand what the pleasure is that streams from the sky in morning light, and what delight that is which the summer breeze brings to my body — when I kiss you to make you smile.

63

THOU hast made me known to friends whom I knew not. Thou hast given me seats in homes not my own. Thou hast brought the distant near and made a brother of the stranger.

I am uneasy at heart when I have to leave my accustomed shelter; I forget that there abides the old in the new, and that there also thou abidest.

Through birth and death, in this world or in others, wherever thou leadest me it is thou, the same, the one companion of my endless life who ever linkest my heart with bonds of joy to the unfamiliar.

When one knows thee, then alien there is none, then no door is shut. Oh, grant me my prayer that I may never lose the bliss of the touch of the one in the play of the many.

64

ON the slope of the desolate river among tall grasses I asked her, "Maiden, where do you go shading your lamp with your mantle? My house is all dark and lonesome — lend me your light!" She raised her dark eyes for a moment and looked at my face through the dusk. "I have come to the river," she said, "to float my lamp on the stream when the daylight wanes in the west." I stood alone among tall grasses and watched the timid flame of her lamp uselessly drifting in the tide.

In the silence of gathering night I asked her, "Maiden, your lights are all lit — then where do you go with your lamp? My house is all dark and lonesome, — lend me your light." She raised her dark eyes on my face and stood for a moment doubtful. "I have come," she said at last, "to dedicate my lamp to the sky." I stood and watched her light uselessly burning in the void.

In the moonless gloom of midnight I asked her, "Maiden, what is your quest holding the lamp near your heart? My house is all dark and lonesome, — lend me your light." She stopped for a minute and thought and gazed at my face in the dark. "I have brought my light," she said, "to join the carnival of lamps." I stood and watched her little lamp uselessly lost among lights.

65

WHAT divine drink wouldst thou have, my God, from this overflowing cup of my life?

My poet, is it thy delight to see thy creation through my eyes and to stand at the portals of my ears silently to listen to thine own eternal harmony?

Thy world is weaving words in my mind and thy joy is adding music to them. Thou givest thyself to me in love and then feelest thine own entire sweetness in me.

66

SHE who ever had remained in the depth of my being, in the twilight of gleams and of glimpses; she who never opened her veils in the morning light, will be my last gift to thee, my God, folded in my final song.

Words have wooed yet failed to win her; persuasion has stretched to her its eager arms in vain.

I have roamed from country to country keeping her in the   core of my heart, and around her have risen and fallen the growth and decay of my life.

Over my thoughts and actions, my slumbers and dreams, she reigned yet dwelled alone and apart.

Many a man knocked at my door and asked for her and turned away in despair.

There was none in the world who ever saw her face to face, and she remained in her loneliness waiting for thy recognition.

67

THOU art the sky and thou art the nest as well.

O thou beautiful, there in the nest it is thy love that encloses the soul with colours and sounds and odours.

There comes the morning with the golden basket in her right hand bearing the wreath of beauty, silently to crown the earth.

And there comes the evening over the lonely meadows deserted by herds, through trackless paths, carrying cool draughts of peace in her golden pitcher from the western ocean of rest.

But there, where spreads the infinite sky for the soul to take her flight in, reigns the stainless white radiance. There is no day nor night, nor form nor colour, and never, never a word.

68

THY sunbeam comes upon this earth of mine with arms outstretched and stands at my door the livelong day to carry back to thy feet clouds made of my tears and sighs and songs.

With fond delight thou wrappest about thy starry breast that mantle of misty cloud, turning it into numberless shapes and folds and colouring it with hues ever changing.

It is so light and so fleeting, tender and tearful and dark, that is why thou lovest it, O thou spotless and serene. And that is why it may cover thy awful white light with its pathetic shadows.

69

THE same stream of life that runs through my veins night and day runs through the world and dances in rhythmic measures.

It is the same life that shoots in joy through the dust of the earth in numberless blades of grass and breaks into tumultuous waves of leaves and flowers.

It is the same life that is rocked in the ocean-cradle of birth and of death, in ebb and in flow.

I feel my limbs are made glorious by the touch of this world of life. And my pride is from the life-throb of ages dancing in my blood this moment.

70

IS it beyond thee to be glad with the gladness of this rhythm? To be tossed and lost and broken in the whirl of this fearful joy?

All things rush on, they stop not, they look not behind, no power can hold them back, they rush on.

Keeping steps with that restless, rapid music, seasons come dancing and pass away — colours, tunes, and perfumes pour in endless cascades in the abounding joy that scatters and gives up and dies every moment.

71

THAT I should make much of myself and turn it on all sides, thus casting coloured shadows on thy radiance — such is thy maya.

Thou settest a barrier in thine own being and then callest thy severed self in myriad notes. This thy self-separation has taken body in me.

The poignant song is echoed through all the sky in many-coloured tears and smiles, alarms and hopes; waves rise up and sink again, dreams break and form. In me is thy own defeat of self.

This screen that thou hast raised is painted with innumerable figures with the brush of the night and the day. Behind it thy seat is woven in wondrous mysteries of curves, casting away all barren lines of straightness.

The great pageant of thee and me has overspread the sky. With the tune of thee and me all the air is vibrant, and all ages pass with the hiding and seeking of thee and me.

72

HE it is, the innermost one, who awakens my being with his deep hidden touches.

He it is who puts his enchantment upon these eyes and joyfully plays on the chords of my heart in varied cadence of pleasure and pain.

He it is who weaves the web of this maya in evanescent hues of gold and silver, blue and green, and lets peep out through the folds his feet, at whose touch I forget myself.

Days come and ages pass, and it is ever he who moves my heart in many a name, in many a guise, in many a rapture of joy and of sorrow.

73

DELIVERANCE is not for me in renunciation. I feel the embrace of freedom in a thousand bonds of delight.

Thou ever pourest for me the fresh draught of thy wine of various colours and fragrance, filling this earthen vessel to the brim.

My world will light its hundred different lamps with thy flame and place them before the altar of thy temple.

No, I will never shut the doors of my senses. The delights of sight and hearing and touch will bear thy delight.

Yes, all my illusions will burn into illumination of joy, and all my desires ripen into fruits of love.

74

THE day is no more, the shadow is upon the earth. It is time that I go to the stream to fill my pitcher.

The evening air is eager with the sad music of the water. Ah, it calls me out into the dusk. In the lonely lane there is no passer by, the wind is up, the ripples are rampant in the river.

I know not if I shall come back home. I know not whom I shall
chance to meet. There at the fording in the little boat the unknown
man plays upon his lute.

75

THY gifts to us mortals fulfil all our needs and yet run back to
thee un-diminished.

The river has its everyday work to do and hastens through fields
and hamlets; yet its incessant stream winds towards the washing
of thy feet.

The flower sweetens the air with its perfume; yet its last service is
to offer itself to thee. Thy worship does not impoverish the world.

From the words of the poet men take what meanings please them;
yet their last meaning points to thee.

76

DAY after DAY, O lord of my life, shall I stand before thee face to
face? With folded hands, O lord of all worlds, shall I stand before
thee face to face?

Under thy great sky in solitude and silence, with humble heart
shall I stand before thee face to face?

In this laborious world of thine, tumultuous with toil and with
struggle, among hurrying crowds shall I stand before thee face
to face?

And when my work shall be done in this world, O King of kings,
alone and speechless shall I stand before thee face to face?

77

I KNOW thee as my God and stand apart — I do not know thee
as my own and come closer. I know thee as my father and bow

before thy feet — I do not grasp thy hand as my friend's.

I stand not where thou comest down and ownest thyself as mine, there to clasp thee to my heart and take thee as my comrade.

Thou art the Brother amongst my brothers, but I heed them not, I divide not my earnings with them, thus sharing my all with thee.

In pleasure and in pain I stand not by the side of men, and thus stand by thee. I shrink to give up my life, and thus do not plunge into the great waters of life.

78

WHEN the creation was new and all the stars shone in their first splendour, the gods held their assembly in the sky and sang "Oh, the picture of perfection! The joy unalloyed!"

But one cried of a sudden — "It seems that somewhere there is a break in the chain of light and one of the stars has been lost."

The golden string of their harp snapped, their song stopped, and they cried in dismay — "Yes, that lost star was the best, she was the glory of all heavens!"

From that day the search is unceasing for her, and the cry goes on from one to the other that in her the world has lost its one joy!

Only in the deepest silence of night the stars smile and whisper among themselves — "Vain is this seeking! Unbroken perfection is over all!"

79

IF it is not my portion to meet thee in this my life then let me ever feel that I have missed thy sight — let me not forget for a moment, let me carry the pangs of this sorrow in my dreams and in my wakeful hours.

As my days pass in the crowded market of this world and my hands grow full with the daily profits, let me ever feel that I have gained nothing — let me not forget for a moment, let me carry the pangs of this sorrow in my dreams and in my wakeful hours.

When I sit by the roadside, tired and panting, when I spread my bed low in the dust, let me ever feel that the long journey is still before me — let me not forget for a moment, let me carry the pangs of this sorrow in my dreams and in my wakeful hours.

When my rooms have been decked out and the flutes sound and the laughter there is loud, let me ever feel that I have not invited thee to my house — let me not forget for a moment, let me carry the pangs of this sorrow in my dreams and in my wakeful hours.

80

I AM like a remnant of a cloud of autumn uselessly roaming in the sky, O my sun ever- glorious! Thy touch has not yet melted my vapour, making me one with thy light, and thus I count months and years separated from thee.

If this be thy wish and if this be thy play, then take this fleeting emptiness of mine, paint it with colours, gild it with gold, float it on the wanton wind and spread it in varied wonders.

And again when it shall be thy wish to end this play at night, I shall melt and vanish away in the dark, or it may be in a smile of the white morning, in a coolness of purity transparent.

81

ON many an idle day have I grieved over lost time. But it is never lost, my lord. Thou hast taken every moment of my life in thine own hands.

Hidden in the heart of things thou art nourishing seeds into sprouts, buds into blossoms, and ripening flowers into fruitfulness.

<h1 style="text-align:center">82</h1>

TIME is endless in thy hands, my lord. There is none to count thy minutes.

Days and nights pass and ages bloom and fade like flowers. Thou knowest how to wait. Thy centuries follow each other perfecting a small wild flower.

We have no time to lose, and having no time we must scramble for our chances. We are too poor to be late.

And thus it is that time goes by while I give it to every querulous man who claims it, and thine altar is empty of all offerings to the last.

At the end of the day I hasten in fear lest thy gate be shut; but I find that yet there is time.

<h1 style="text-align:center">83</h1>

MOTHER, I shall weave a chain of pearls for thy neck with my tears of sorrow.

The stars have wrought their anklets of light to deck thy feet, but mine will hang upon thy breast.

Wealth and fame come from thee and it is for thee to give or to withhold them. But this my sorrow is absolutely mine own, and when I bring it to thee as my offering thou rewardest me with thy grace.

<h1 style="text-align:center">84</h1>

IT is the pang of separation that spreads throughout the world and gives birth to shapes innumerable in the infinite sky.

It is this sorrow of separation that gazes in silence all night from star to star and becomes lyric among rustling leaves in rainy darkness of July.

It is this overspreading pain that deepens into loves and desires, into sufferings and joys in human homes; and this it is that ever melts and flows in songs through my poet's heart.

85

WHEN the warriors came out first from their master's hall, where had they hid their power? Where were their armour and their arms?

They looked poor and helpless, and the arrows were showered upon them on the day they came out from their master's hall.

When the warriors marched back again to their master's hall where did they hide their power?

They had dropped the sword and dropped the bow and the arrow; peace was on their foreheads, and they had left the fruits of their life behind them on the day they marched back again to their master's hall.

86

DEATH, thy servant, is at my door. He has crossed the unknown sea and brought thy call to my home.

The night is dark and my heart is fearful yet I will take up the lamp, open my gates and bow to him my welcome. It is thy messenger who stands at my door.

I will worship him with folded hands, and with tears. I will worship him placing at his feet the treasure of my heart.

He will go back with his errand done, leaving a dark shadow on my morning; and in my desolate home only my forlorn self will remain as my last offering to thee.

87

IN desperate hope I go and search for her in all the corners of my room; I find her not.

My house is small and what once has gone from it can never be regained. But infinite is thy mansion, my lord, and seeking her I have come to thy door. I stand under the golden canopy of thine evening sky and I lift my eager eyes to thy face.

I have come to the brink of eternity from which nothing can vanish — no hope, no happiness, no vision of a face seen through tears.

Oh, dip my emptied life into that ocean, plunge it into the deepest fullness.

Let me for once feel that lost sweet touch in the allness of the universe.

88

DEITY of the ruined temple! The broken strings of Vina sing no more your praise. The bells in the evening proclaim not your time of worship. The air is still and silent about you.

In your desolate dwelling comes the vagrant spring breeze. It brings the tidings of flowers — the flowers that for your worship are offered no more.

Your worshipper of old wanders ever longing for favour still refused. In the eventide, when fires and shadows mingle with the gloom of dust, he wearily comes back to the ruined temple with hunger in his heart.

Many a festival day comes to you in silence, deity of the ruined temple. Many a night of worship goes away with lamp unlit.

Many new images are built by masters of cunning art and carried to the holy stream of oblivion when their time is come.

Only the deity of the ruined temple remains unworshipped in deathless neglect.

89

NO more noisy, loud words from me — such is my master's will.
Henceforth I deal in whispers. The speech of my heart will be
carried on in murmurings of a song.

Men hasten to the King's market. All the buyers and sellers are
there. But I have my untimely leave in the middle of the day, in the
thick of work.

Let then the flowers come out in my garden, though it is not their
time and let the midday bees strike up their lazy hum.

Full many an hour have I spent in the strife of the good and the
evil, but now it is the pleasure of my playmate of the empty days to
draw my heart on to him; and I know not why is this sudden call
to what useless inconsequence!

90

ON the day when death will knock at thy door what wilt thou
offer to him?

Oh, I will set before my guest the full vessel of my life — I will
never let him go with empty hands.

All the sweet vintage of all my autumn days and summer nights,
all the earnings and gleanings of my busy life will I place before
him at the close of my days when death will knock at my door.

91

O THOU the last fulfilment of life, Death, my death, come and
whisper to me!

Day after day have I kept watch for thee; for thee have I borne the
joys and pangs of life.

All that I am, that I have, that I hope and all my love have ever
flowed towards thee in depth of secrecy. One final glance from
thine eyes and my life will be ever thine own.

The flowers have been woven and the garland is ready for the bridegroom. After the wedding the bride shall leave her home and meet her lord alone in the solitude of night.

92

I KNOW that the day will come when my sight of this earth shall be lost, and life will take its leave in silence, drawing the last curtain over my eyes.

Yet stars will watch at night, and morning rise as before, and hours heave like sea waves casting up pleasures and pains.

When I think of this end of my moments, the barrier of the moments breaks and I see by the light of death thy world with its careless treasures. Rare is its lowliest seat, rare is its meanest of lives.

Things that I longed for in vain and things that I got — let them pass. Let me but truly possess the things that I ever spurned and overlooked.

93

I HAVE got my leave. Bid me farewell, my brothers! I bow to you all and take my departure.

Here I give back the keys of my door — and I give up all claims to my house. I only ask for last kind words from you.

We were neighbours for long, but I received more than I could give. Now the day has dawned and the lamp that lit my dark corner is out. A summons has come and I am ready for my journey.

94

AT this time of my parting, wish me good luck, my friends! The sky is flushed with the dawn and my path lies beautiful.

Ask not what I have with me to take there. I start on my journey with empty hands and expectant heart.

I shall put on my wedding garland. Mine is not the red-brown dress of the traveller, and though there are dangers on the way I have no fear in my mind.

The evening star will come out when my voyage is done and the plaintive notes of the twilight melodies be struck up from the King's gateway.

95

I WAS not aware of the moment when I first crossed the threshold of this life.

What was the power that made me open out into this vast mystery like a bud in the forest at midnight!

When in the morning I looked upon the light I felt in a moment that I was no stranger in this world, that the inscrutable without name and form had taken me in its arms in the form of my own mother.

Even so, in death the same unknown will appear as ever known to me. And because I love this life, I know I shall love death as well.

The child cries out when from the right breast the mother takes it away, in the very next moment to find in the left one its consolation.

96

WHEN I go from hence let this be my parting word, that what I have seen is unsurpassable.

I have tasted of the hidden honey of this lotus that expands on the ocean of light, and thus am I blessed — let this be my parting word.

In this playhouse of infinite forms I have had my play and here have I caught sight of him that is formless.

My whole body and my limbs have thrilled with his touch who is beyond touch; and if the end comes here, let it come — let this be my parting word.

97

WHEN my play was with thee I never questioned who thou wert. I knew nor shyness nor fear, my life was boisterous.

In the early morning thou wouldst call me from my sleep like my own comrade and lead me running from glade to glade.

On those days I never cared to know the meaning of songs thou sangest to me. Only my voice took up the tunes, and my heart danced in their cadence.

Now, when the playtime is over, what is this sudden sight that is come upon me? The world with eyes bent upon thy feet stands in awe with all its silent stars.

98

I WILL deck thee with trophies, garlands of my defeat. It is never in my power to escape unconquered.

I surely know my pride will go to the wall, my life will burst its bonds in exceeding pain, and my empty heart will sob out in music like a hollow reed, and the stone will melt in tears.

I surely know the hundred petals of a lotus will not remain closed for ever and the secret recess of its honey will be bared.

From the blue sky an eye shall gaze upon me and summon me in silence. Nothing will be left for me, nothing whatever, and utter death shall I receive at thy feet.

99

WHEN I give up the helm I know that the time has come for thee to take it. What there is to do will be instantly done. Vain is this struggle.

Then take away your hands and silently put up with your defeat, my heart, and think it your good fortune to sit perfectly still where you are placed.

These my lamps are blown out at every little puff of wind, and trying to light them I forget all else again and again.

But I shall be wise this time and wait in the dark, spreading my mat on the floor; and whenever it is thy pleasure, my lord, come silently and take thy seat here.

100

I DIVE down into the depth of the ocean of forms, hoping to gain the perfect pearl of the formless.

No more sailing from harbour to harbour with this my weather-beaten boat. The days are long passed when my sport was to be tossed on waves.

And now I am eager to die into the deathless.

Into the audience hall by the fathomless abyss where swells up the music of toneless strings I shall take this harp of my life.

I shall tune it to the notes of for ever, and, when it has sobbed out its last utterance, lay down my silent harp at the feet of the silent.

101

EVER in my life have I sought thee with my songs. It was they who led me from door to door, and with them have I felt about me, searching and touching my world.

It was my songs that taught me all the lessons I ever learnt; they showed me secret paths, they brought before my sight many a star on the horizon of my heart.

They guided me all the day long to the mysteries of the country of pleasure and pain, and, at last, to what palace gate have they brought me in the evening at the end of my journey?

102

BOASTED among men that I had known you. They see your pictures in all works of mine. They come and ask me, "Who is he?" I know not how to answer them. I say, "Indeed, I cannot tell." They blame me and they go away in scorn. And you sit there smiling.

I put my tales of you into lasting songs. The secret gushes out from my heart. They come and ask me, "Tell me all your meanings." I know not how to answer them. I say, "Ah, who knows what they mean!" They smile and go away in utter scorn. And you sit there smiling.

103

IN one salutation to thee, my God, let all my senses spread out and touch this world at thy feet.

Like a rain-cloud of July hung low with its burden of unshed showers let all my mind bend down at thy door in one salutation to thee.

Let all my songs gather together their diverse strains into a single current and flow to a sea of silence in one salutation to thee.

Like a flock of homesick cranes flying night and day back to their mountain nests let all my life take its voyage to its eternal home in one salutation to thee.

Acknowledgements

I thank the editors of the following journals where some of these poems were first published, at times in earlier versions: *The Charles River Journal* (ed. Medha Singh); *RELIQUIAE, Vol 8 No 2* (eds. Autumn Richardson and Richard Skelton); and *Beltway Poetry Quarterly* (ed. Indran Amirthanayagam).

In Br, Himachal Pradesh: Sunanda and Anil Dikonda of Avva's Café where this book began as a riffle of the *Gitanjali's* pages over superb filter coffee. The Pal family, royal hoteliers and friends, whose idyllic Colonel's Resort became, for a month, my writing retreat.

I thank Jojy Philip for impeccably laying out a 'floating' text, and designer Gavin Morris for wonderfully revisioning Katsushika Hokusai's woodblock print of the sacred Kikifuri waterfall on Mt Kurokami as the cover design. My heartfelt thanks to V. K. Karthika, who welcomed this book, and for the imagination, élan and precision she brings to the editorial process.

I thank friends who have been invaluable fellow travellers on this journey. In particular, Bhaswati Ghosh, for her astute comments on the introductory essay; Sucharita Dutta-Asane, first reader, for her warm and thoughtful responses; Ranjit Hoskote, for sharing his illuminating essay on Tagore and his generous response to excerpts that lifted my spirits; and George Szirtes, whose insightful observations on matters poetic were once again there for me, as they have been for over two decades.

As always, my deepest gratitude to my husband, Suresh Chabria, for his inspiring companionship and unwavering support. Without him, this book—and much that is beauteous in my life—would not be.